A New Owner's
Guide to
SAINT BERNARDS

JG 161

Overleaf: Saint Bernard photographed by Isabelle Francais

Opposite Page: Saint Bernard photographed by Isabelle Francais

The Publisher wishes to acknowledge the owners of the dogs in this book: Dianne Bowen, Arlene and Dick Buck, Don and Marcia Carter, Vicki Cliff, Davetta Curtiss, Patrick Dionne, Don and Carole Dvorak, Mike and Cathy Figueroa, Tony Genovese, Jerri Hobbs, Jamie Johnson, Tyrol Kennels, Patricia Kinser, Deborah Lauber, Tina McIllveene, Geneva Murray, Elisabeth Nelson, Patty Neumayer, Bill and Diana Oliver, Michael Parker, Jerry and Sue Parliman, Arthur and Gary Raike, Melody Robinson, Terry and Becky Shaw, Betty-Anne Stenmark, Melissa Wirkkala

Photographers: Martin Booth, Dianne Bowen, Don and Marcia Carter, Don and Carole Dvorak, Isabelle Francais, Jerri Hobbs, Patricia Kinser, Jayne Langdon, Tina McIllveene, Johnnie McMillan, Geneva Murray, Bill and Diana Oliver, Robert Pearcy, Pets by Paulette, Terry and Becky Shaw, Betty-Anne Stenmark

The author acknowledges the contribution of Judy Iby for the following chapters in this book: Sport of Purebred Dogs, Health Care, Identification and Finding the Lost Dog, Traveling with Your Dog, and Behavior and Canine Communication.

The portrayal of canine pet products in this book is for general instructive value only; the appearance of such products does not necessarily constitute an endorsement by the authors, the publisher, or the owners of the dogs portrayed in this book.

Distributed in the UNITED STATES to the Pet Trade by T.F.H. Publications, Inc., 1 TFH Plaza, Neptune City, NJ 07753; on the Internet at www.tfh.com; in CANADA by Rolf C. Hagen Inc., 3225 Sartelon St., Montreal, Quebec H4R 1E8; Pet Trade by H & L Pet Supplies Inc., 27 Kingston Crescent, Kitchener, Ontario N2B 2T6; in ENGLAND by T.F.H. Publications, PO Box 74, Havant PO9 5TT; in AUSTRALIA AND THE SOUTH PACIFIC by T.F.H. (Australia), Pty. Ltd., Box 149, Brookvale 2100 N.S.W., Australia; in NEW ZEALAND by Brooklands Aquarium Ltd., 5 McGiven Drive, New Plymouth, RD1 New Zealand; in SOUTH AFRICA by Rolf C. Hagen S.A. (PTY.) LTD., P.O. Box 201199, Durban North 4016, South Africa; in JAPAN by T.F.H. Publications. Published by T.F.H. Publications, Inc.

MANUFACTURED IN THE
UNITED STATES OF AMERICA
BY T.F.H. PUBLICATIONS, INC.

A NEW OWNER'S GUIDE TO
SAINT BERNARDS

BETTY-ANNE STENMARK

Contents

6 · Origin and History of the Saint Bernard
The Saint Bernard Comes to America

The adorable face and loving personality of the Saint Bernard puppy is often hard to resist.

16 · Characteristics of the Saint Bernard
Case for the Purebred Puppy • Who Should Own a Saint Bernard? • Character of the Saint Bernard

26 · Standard for the Saint Bernard
Shorthaired • Longhaired

32 · Selecting the Right Saint Bernard for You
What to Look for in a Breeder • Health Concerns • Questions and Answers • Recognizing a Healthy Puppy • Male or Female? • Selecting a Show-Prospect Puppy • Puppy or Adult? • Identification Papers • Diet Sheet • Health Guarantee • Temperament and Socialization • The Adolescent Saint Bernard

The Saint Bernard is a trainable breed that enjoys spending quality time with his owner.

54 · Caring for Your Saint Bernard
Feeding and Nutrition • Bathing and Grooming • Exercise • Socialization

64 · Housebreaking and Training Your Saint Bernard
Housebreaking Made Easy • Basic Training • Training Classes • Fun and Games

A gentle giant, the affectionate Saint Bernard makes a wonderful companion for children.

128 · Traveling with Your Dog
Trips • Air Travel • Boarding Kennels

134 · Identification and Finding the Lost Dog
Finding the Lost Dog

The obedient Saint Bernard is well known for his amazing search and rescue abilities.

82 · Sport of Purebred Dogs
Puppy Kindergarten • Conformation • Canine Good Citizen • Obedience • Tracking • Agility • Performance Tests

104 · Health Care
The First Checkup • The Physical Exam • Immunizations • Annual Visit • Intestinal Parasites • Other Internal Parasites • External Parasites • To Breed or Not To Breed

122 · Dental Care for Your Dog's Life

These tiny Saint Bernard puppies will grow into massive adult dogs with fun-loving personalities.

138 · Behavior and Canine Communication
Canine Behavior • Socializing and Training • Understanding the Dog's Language • Body Language • Fear • Aggression • Problems

159 · Suggested Reading

160 · Index

ORIGIN and History of the Saint Bernard

While the histories of most purebred dogs are mired in obscurity, a great deal is known about the beginnings of the Saint Bernard breed. Of course, some of it is left to speculation, but thanks to the good monks of the Hospice of Grand Saint Bernard and several early breeders—most notably Herr Heinrich Schumacher—a great deal of the early history of the breed was recorded.

The Hospice of Grand Saint Bernard is usually credited with being the birthplace of the Saint Bernard, but breeders in the valley areas around the isolated hospice are probably the progenitors of the breed. It is logical that the early dogs were gifts to the monks from the local nobility and aristocracy. There is no mention in the hospice archives of so-called "service dogs" being kept at the hospice before the second half of the 17th century. However, two paintings by an Italian artist at the hospice dated 1695 are of two short-haired, heavily built, mastiff-type dogs, easily recognized as early representatives of the Saint Bernard breed. Scholars of the breed believe the dogs came to the hospice between 1660 and 1670, and by the time of those paintings, through selection for three or four decades for certain characteristics, the breed evolved and the "hospice type" was set.

Ch. Revilio's Quincy, owned by Bill and Diana Oliver, participating in the 1999 S.B.C.A. National Specialty Draft Test.

In Albert de la Rie's book, *The Saint Bernard Classic*, numerous anecdotes are compiled from the period 1774 to 1827 documenting some of the escapades of the monks and their dogs. The earliest of these anecdotes is the second

Much about the Saint Bernard is known, thanks to the monks of the Hospice of Grand Saint Bernard—the birthplace of the Saint Bernard. Saint puppies owned by Don and Carole Dvorak.

recorded mention of the breed, when M. J. Bourrit wrote in a letter from the hospice about a hospice dog aiding travelers in an avalanche: "Dogs of extraordinary size were trained to help travelers or to serve as guides. Many times, during snowstorms and fog, the dogs perished." The hospice is located at the highest point in the Great Saint Bernard Pass, 8,000 feet above sea level, and in those days it was the route taken by travelers going from Switzerland to Northern Italy. Snow is recorded there 9 months of the year, and the average annual snowfall is 36 feet, making travel by foot treacherous indeed.

In 1787, the hospice dogs performed a different function from their normal rescue work, displaying the Saint's natural abilities to guard his home and family: In the hospice's records is a note about the dogs protecting the hospice from a gang of burglars.

In 1780, J. B. Laborde and F.A. de Zurlauben of Paris described the dogs' rescue work in a letter: "The monks who daily searched for people in danger during the eight or nine most dangerous months are accompanied by very large trained dogs who track down injured or lost persons and help them out of their emergencies by guiding them to the Monastery."

A member of the University of Oxford writes in *Alpine Sketches* of his trip over the pass in the summer of 1814 and of the wonderful capacity of the hospice dogs—how they find lost travelers buried in snow, arouse them, and lead them to the monastery. Further, he mentions that the dogs carry a small wine barrel around their necks. These three descriptions are representative of the many notes written by people who visited the hospice during the development of the Saint Bernard breed.

From 1800 to 1814 lived one of the most famous of the early Saints. His name was Barry and his heroics were legendary—he was said to have saved 40 lives. From the Museum of Natural History in Switzerland, we learn that Barry performed his duties for 12 years before retiring to a farm near Bern in 1813. After his death in 1814, he was stuffed and is still displayed at the Museum today.

It was about the time of Barry that the British became interested in the hospice dogs, and Britain's most prominent animal artist of the times, Sir Edwin Landseer, (1802-1873) painted the Saint that appeared in the Swiss stud book as "No. 5." This dog, known as "Lion," was all one color, a reddish-yellow with only a small white strip on the bridge of the muzzle. Lion had been sold to England and Landseer painted him when the dog was about 12 months old. He reportedly stood 31 inches at the top of the shoulder, considered as tall then as it would be today. Copies of Sir Edwin's portrait were made and the work was called "Alpine Mastiff," the name most often used by the British at the time. The Saint Bernard enjoyed considerable popularity in England through the latter half of the 19th century. The British Saint was of a different type from the rest of the world, favoring a flatter narrower head and a more willowy frame.

The original stock were all short-haired and remained so up until 1830, at which time it's thought that the Newfoundland was bred to the Saint Bernard. From this cross came the long-haired or rough-coated variety. The cross was made in the erroneous belief that the long hair would provide more warmth to the dogs working in the snowy and icy conditions of the high pass. However, the long hair proved to be a detriment. When the dogs were wading through snow drifts, the long-haired Saints became covered with ice and snow, hindering their work as mountain rescue dogs. When the unsuitability of the long-haired dogs for rescue work became obvious, the monks gave the long-haired pups away to friends in the valleys, keeping only the short-haired pups at the monastery. It should be noted that the 1830 date is debatable, because the first written documentation of Newfoundland dogs at the Hospice wasn't until 1856, when Prior J. Deleglise reported that two Newfoundlands had been brought from Stuttgart, Germany, for training as rescue dogs.

It was the original belief that the long-haired Saints would be more protected in the harsh weather than the short-haired Saints. However, the longer hair proved to be a detriment in the snow and ice.

The monastery was founded in 1049 by Holy Saint Bernard de Menthon. On his death in 1081, the mountaintop on which he'd built his monastery was named for him. It was inevitable that the dogs later kept at the monastery would eventually take on this name too, but like so many other breeds, the Saint was known by numerous names before settling on Saint Bernard. They were at times called "Hospice Dogs," "Barry Dogs," "Bernhardiner," "Holy Dogs," "Cloister Dogs," and "Alpine Mastiffs."

Long-haired Ch. Ludwig v. Slade was a consistent winner on the West Coast in the 1960s, shown here by Roy Stenmark.

Heinrich Schumacher (1831-1903) began breeding Saint Bernards between 1855 and 1860. He, along with the hospice monks and a few valley residents, did much of the foundation breeding, and through selection for certain characteristics, a type was set. Herr Schumacher is credited with being the best of these early breeders, and his knowledge of breeding practices appeared to be well ahead of his day. He donated dogs to the hospice, including two of his best. One of these was said to have been of "Barry" type, the type he thought ideal. Schumacher retired in 1890, giving his dogs to Herr Muller in Brig and Herr Seiler in Zermatt. His line continued to be an important influence.

The Swiss Kennel Club was founded in 1883 to protect the Saint Bernard from the English enthusiasts who had adopted their own Saint standard the previous year. In 1884, the SKC adopted the Swiss Saint Bernard standard, which was the work of, among others, Herr Schumacher. An International Congress was held in Belgium in 1886 and the Swiss delegates, Saint Bernard breeders Dr. T. Kunzli and Dr. B. Siegmund, defended the Swiss standard against the English version. Nothing decisive came from this conference, but at meetings held during the International Show in Zurich in June 1887, the Swiss standard was accepted by representatives of all nations attending, except the English. Today, as then, the British Isles are the only countries that do not embrace the Swiss standard.

Although the short-haired Saint Bernard was the original variety for many years, around 1913, more people began leaning toward the long-haired dogs. Two short-haired pups, owned by Dianne Bowen.

The first Swiss dog show was held in Bern in 1871, and here the Swiss type was promoted. Herr Schumacher's dogs won most of the prizes, with firsts going to Barry II, Sultan II, and Favorite II. It wasn't until 1881 that another show was held, at which 200 Saint Bernards were shown, a large entry at any time in Saint Bernard history. Shows were again held in 1872, where no first prizes were awarded, and in 1873, where Herr Schumacher also deemed no exhibit worthy of a First Prize.

The first Swiss Dog stud book was published in 1884, and 13 short-haired and 14 long-haired Saints were registered. The four breeders included Herr Schumacher and Dr. Kunzli.

The year 1905 marked the first mention of the titles of Sieger and Siegerin. The Sieger award may be given to as many as four dogs each year at the equivalent of the Swiss National Specialty Show. One award for each sex in each coat variety is allowed, although at the option of the judge, the award may also be withheld if the winners are not of sufficient high quality.

For many years, the balance of short-haired and long-haired dogs kept by Saint breeders was roughly equal, but around 1913, the balance tipped in favor of the long-haired variety. There was great concern among breeders, because the short-haired dog was the original variety, and most felt that the best type was obtained by breeding short-haired to long-haired dogs. Because the long-haired gene is recessive, when long-hair is bred to long-hair, only long-haired offspring result. The great Dutch breed historian and authority, Albert de la Rie, wrote in the early 1970s, "The fear is...unknowledgeable breeders who would persist in breeding rough to rough for many generations and thereby lose type. It is a basic fundamental that the smooth blood must be blended with the rough on a regular basis or the basic type will truly deteriorate." Most long-time breeders of Saints realize this statement to be true, and in general, the very best type today is still in the short-haired specimens.

During World War II, most dog breeding was put on hold. However, the Saint suffered less than most other breeds due to Switzerland remaining neutral in the hostilities.

THE SAINT BERNARD COMES TO AMERICA

The late 1920s saw the birth of two dogs: a great sire, Sg. Emir v. Jura and his equally impressive son, Rasko v.d. Reppisch, both of whom contributed greatly to the quality of Saints in Europe as well as America. Rasko won the Swiss Sieger titles in 1931 and 1932 and was the winner of the first National Specialty in America held in 1935. He was imported by Paul Forbriger of the Waldeck Kennels in New York State, and later was sold to Norman F. Keller of Tall Maples Kennels.

Dog breeding everywhere was on hold during World War II, but with Switzerland remaining neutral in the hostilities, it seems that the Saint Bernard suffered less than most other

Sweepstakes class winners under Mrs. Lillian Buell, owner of the famous Subira Kennels, at the 1975 Saint Bernard Club of the Pacific Coast Specialty. Castor's Cameo of Tyrol and Tyrol's Melody Double Castor.

breeds in the Western World. After the war Gerd v.d. Lueg was born and imported to America in 1946 and sold to Joseph H. Fleischli, Jr., of Edelweiss Kennels in Illinois. Gerd won the Saint Bernard Club of America (SBCA) National Specialty in three consecutive years (1950, 1951, and 1952) and racked up an impressive 21 all-breed Bests in Show. His litter sister, Gerda v.d. Lueg, was imported by Mr. and Mrs. A. F. Hayes of Alpine Plateau Kennels in Portland, Oregon, and won Best of Breed at the 1948 SBCA National Specialty with her brother, Gerd, going Best of Opposite Sex.

In 1950, another important dog, Faust v. Melina, was exported to Irwin Cohn. This dog was later sold to Stanley Bussinger of Highmont Kennels in Pennsylvania. Faust was the winner of the 1956 SBCA National Specialty. Faust would prove to be quite an influence on the Shagg-Bark line of the Roberts in Connecticut, siring their Ch. Frieda's Al-ver-don Frausty. In the late '50s, the Subira Kennels of the Buells in California enjoyed much

Ch. Banz v. Schwandenblick, the top winner in Europe in 1969, standing in the garden of Hans Zimmerli of Langenthal, the president of the Saint Bernard Breeders' Association.

success from a Frausty daughter, Ch. Nelda of Birchwood, who would become the top producing Saint bitch in history with 22 champion offspring, a record that still stands today. Her son, Ch. Subira's Casper The Viking was the top winner in the late '60s. Casper was owned by Eleanor Keaton, wife of the famous comic actor Buster Keaton. Another Nelda son, Ch. San Subira, was the top obedience sire in the history of the breed. Nelda produced not only beauty, but brains.

In 1951, another prominent dog arrived in America, Banz v. Bachingerhof, and he found his way to the Sanctuary Woods Kennels of Beatrice Knight, in Drain, Oregon. Mrs. Knight's kennels produced countless winners and producers, the names of Better Times, Deep Thought, Fantabulous, Four Winds, Gulliver, and others being legendary in the breed. Mrs. Knight's location was quite isolated, and she was able to keep large numbers of dogs and bred extensively. Her line figures prominently in the pedigrees of many of today's Saints.

The early Swiss Imports were used wisely and can be found in the background of most of the best Saints in Canada and the United States.

In the late '60s, the Saint Bernard specialties were dominated by two rough-coats. One was Ch. Titan v. Mallen, whelped in 1963 and bred and owned by Lou Mallen of New Jersey. Titan was a great-grandson of Faust v. Melina and a great-great-grandson of Gerd v.d. Lueg. The other was Ch. Sanctuary Woods Kleona, whelped in 1968, bred and owned by Beatrice Knight and co-owned by Robert and Mary Tarlton. Kleona was a granddaughter of Banz v. Bachingerhof.

Titan and Kleona, while bred on opposite coasts, were of similar type and widely admired in Saint circles. They have had profound influence on the breed today. They both had very impressive heads with great width of skull, heavy bodies, lots of angulation front and rear, and heavy bone. While massive, they were not tall. This type has continued in America and is quite different from the dogs originally imported from Switzerland and those that were bred here up until the late '60s.

A gentle giant, the Saint Bernard makes a wonderful companion. Be sure that your living conditions can accommodate this huge breed.

Swiss Imports would continue to have influence in America, but the 1960s saw the emergence of top-winning and producing American-bred Saint Bernards. The kennel names of Powell, Riga, Stanridge, Harvey's, Shagg-Bark, Subira, Mardonof, Alpenhof, Dawrob, Beau Cheval, Sanctuary Woods, Prairieaire, von Mallen, Templehof, Saints Retreat, Madonna, Engler, High Chateau, and others dominated the show rings through the heydays of the breed, the '60s and '70s. It was not uncommon for an average show to have an entry of 100 Saints and the National Specialty would draw in excess of 350 dogs. Today, most local shows have only a few Saints exhibited, and there are less than 200 at the National Specialty. This is not a bad thing, because seldom is quality equated with quantity. The Saint is a wonderful companion and a great all-around family dog, but a giant breed is certainly not meant to fit into the average household.

CHARACTERISTICS of the Saint Bernard

All puppies are cuddly and cute. The Saint baby is cute beyond words—with his black mask, adoring eyes, oversized feet, and large size, he has a special charm that is hard to resist. There is nothing more adorable than a litter of little puppies, nestled together sound asleep, one on top of the other. But in addition to being cute, puppies are living, breathing, extremely mischievous creatures that are entirely dependent upon their human owner for everything once they leave their mother and littermates. Furthermore, the innocent-appearing, dependent little Saint puppy that weighs around 20 pounds when you take him home grows by leaps and bounds, quickly becoming a very large and gawky adolescent.

Buying a dog, especially a Saint puppy, before you are absolutely sure that you want to make that commitment can be a serious mistake. The prospective dog

With their sleepy eyes and oversized feet, Saint puppies are often hard to resist. Be aware of the breed's characteristics and special needs before purchasing a puppy.

Puppies take up a lot of your time and energy, so make sure that the decision to bring one into your home has been carefully considered.
owner must clearly understand the amount of time and work involved in the ownership of any dog. Failure to understand the extent of commitment involved is one of the primary reasons that so many unwanted canines end their lives in an animal shelter.

Before anyone contemplates the purchase of a dog, there are some very important considerations. One of the first important questions that must be answered is whether or not the person who will ultimately be responsible for the dog's care and well-being actually wants a dog.

If the prospective dog owner lives alone, all she needs to do is be sure that she has a strong desire to make the necessary commitment dog ownership entails. In the case of family households, it is vital that the person who will ultimately be responsible for the dog's care really wants a dog.

Pets are a wonderful method of teaching children responsibility, but it should be remembered that the enthusiasm that inspires children to promise anything in order to have a new puppy may quickly wane. Keep in mind that the adult Saint Bernard may be too powerful a dog for a child to handle. Nowadays, mothers, too, are out in the workplace, but all too often they are saddled with the additional chores of feeding and trips to the veterinary hospital with what was supposed to be a family project.

The Saint's loving and gentle nature makes him a great playmate for easygoing children.

Desire to own a dog aside, does the lifestyle of the family actually provide for responsible dog ownership? If the entire family is away from home from early morning to late at night, who will provide for all of the puppy's needs? Feeding, exercise, outdoor access, and the like cannot be provided if no one is home.

Another important factor to consider is whether or not the breed of dog is suitable for the person or the family with which he will be living. Some breeds can handle the rough-and-tumble play of young children, and some cannot. On the other hand, some dogs are so large and clumsy, especially as puppies, that they could easily and unintentionally injure an infant.

You must also consider grooming requiremens. A luxuriously coated dog is certainly beautiful to behold, but all that hair takes care. In the case of a Saint, even the short-haired variety has an undercoat, and they, like the long-haired variety, shed their coats in the home. Daily use of a vacuum cleaner is a must in the household of a Saint Bernard.

Excess salivation is another issue concerning the breed. You have undoubtedly heard about the so-called "dry mouth" Saint Bernards. While some Saints have more flew than others (the flew, or folds of flesh hanging from the dog's mouth, is the catch-basin for the dog's saliva), the fact remains that the breed does drool—some dogs more than others. When a Saint stands up and shakes his head, drool can be flung as far as the wall across the room, up on the ceiling, or on your nice, clean sports jacket. Devoted Saint Bernard owners ignore this minor nuisance, keeping a small towel nearby to clean up such mishaps. However, to some discriminating housekeepers, this

aspect of Saint ownership may present a problem. It's best to discuss all this before buying the puppy.

As great as claims are for any breed's intelligence and trainability, remember that the new dog must be taught every household rule that he is to observe. Some dogs catch on more quickly than others, and puppies are just as inclined to forget or disregard lessons as young human children.

CASE FOR THE PUREBRED PUPPY

Not all puppies, however cute they may be, grow up to be particularly attractive adults. It is almost impossible to determine what a mixed-breed puppy will look like as an adult, nor will it be possible to determine if the mixed-breed puppy's temperament is suitable for the person or family who wishes to own him. If the puppy grows up to be too big or too active for the owner, what will happen to him?

Despite the Saint's natural intelligence and trainability, he must be taught every household rule that you wish him to follow.

Size and temperament can vary to a degree even within a purebred dog. Still, selective breeding over many generations has produced dogs that give the would-be owner reasonable assurance of what the purebred puppy will look and act like as an adult. This predictability is more important than one might think.

A person who wants a dog to go along on those morning jogs or long-distance runs is not going to be particularly happy with a lethargic or short-legged breed. Nor is the fastidious housekeeper, whose picture of the ideal dog is one that lies quietly at the feet of his master by the hour and never sheds, going to be particularly happy with the shaggy dog whose temperament is reminiscent of a hurricane.

Purebred puppies will grow up to look like their adult relatives, and by and large they will behave pretty much like

The Saint Bernard enjoys his role as family guardian and protector. Here, Swissongs Morning Glory, owned by Terry and Becky Shaw, takes a break from his duties.

the rest of their family. Any dog, mixed breed or not, has the potential to be a loving companion. However, a purebred dog offers reasonable insurance that it will not only suit the owner's lifestyle but the person's aesthetic demands as well.

WHO SHOULD OWN A SAINT BERNARD?

The Saint Bernard is a multipurpose dog. For the family, he fulfills the traditional role of companion and guardian to adults as well as children. He enjoys participating in whatever the family is doing, and keeps a watchful eye over each member of the family.

A working couple can make a good home for a Saint Bernard provided that when they are at home, the dog is not left outside but is included whenever possible in the evening and weekend activities. He needs to feel like he is a full-fledged member of the family.

Provisions must be made for the Saint puppy when the family is away from home. Rather than leaving a puppy or teenager loose in the house, unattended, it is best that a safe outdoor enclosure be made for him. A fenced yard works, but if you enjoy gardening, flowers, and shrubs, a puppy who likes to do some gardening on his own is not going to make you happy. A fenced dog run, tucked away on the side of the house or at the end of the garden, where he can still see his family, can be the puppy's home away from home.

A 10-foot by 40-foot space is enough, although larger is better still, and the run should be enclosed with 6-foot cyclone fencing. Small-size gravel several inches deep will keep the dog clean, and a large dog house located at one end will protect him from the elements. A manger of straw makes a great bed in the dog house, which is preferable over soft blankets. Providing a soft surface for your Saint to sleep on is important, because giant breeds tend to drop themselves down heavily, causing calluses and bursas on their elbows and hocks.

For members of the family who have an interest in traditional obedience work or agility competitions, the Saint Bernard has proven to be a competent competitor. While never exhibiting the quick precision work of breeds like the Doberman Pinscher or the Shetland Sheepdog, the Saint has proven he can earn every title available within the sport.

For the family that enjoys the outdoors, the Saint is an ideal dog. He enjoys "carting"—pulling a cart like a small draft horse. If you live in an area where it snows in the winter, the Saint loves to pull a sled. He is also a willing pack animal, and canine-style backpacks are available for dogs of his size. This is a wonderful way to pack the family picnic lunch on a hike into the mountains. Many Saint Bernard clubs also offer weight-pulling competitions, and titles are awarded to the winners at these events.

With the Saint's history, it is no surprise that they are still used today in search and rescue operations. Their hearing and scent abilities are keen, and just as they did more than two centuries ago, the Saint can still rescue trapped humans.

One of the most frequently asked questions of a Saint owner is, "How much does he weigh?" His size—standing an average of 27 inches at the top of the shoulder and weighing at maturity approximately 150 pounds—makes a commanding presence in your home, as well as your automobile. No, you don't have to have a station wagon or minivan to transport your dog, but it's a good idea. A full-grown Saint occupies the same space as a human member of your family. Despite the appearance that he is an ideal outdoor dog, the Saint thrives by being with his special people wherever they are, indoors or out.

A Saint Bernard requires a lot of socialization, obedience classes through puppyhood and adolescence, and excursions to the grocery store, the schoolyard, and the park. He loves to ride in the car, wherever you're going. While he enjoys a long walk, due to his extraordinary size and rapid growth, he must be conditioned slowly and sensibly before he is exposed to vigorous exercise.

History records show that Saint Bernards were used as rescue dogs. Today, because of their acute hearing and scent abilities, they are still doing a great job.

CHARACTER OF THE SAINT BERNARD

The word "noble" is nowhere in the written standard of excellence of the Saint Bernard, but fanciers through the years have always used the word when speaking of the

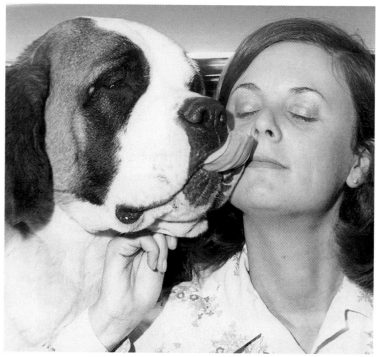

The Saint Bernard projects confidence and strength, yet gentleness and warmth. Here, the author gets a huge hello. breed. His look, carriage, and whole being is one of self-confidence. He is reliable—a dog that can be trusted no matter what the circumstances. A Saint is calm and placid yet alert and inquisitive. He is always friendly and interested in his surroundings.

Through the years, the breed has inspired total loyalty on the part of its supporters. A Saint Bernard owner is usually a Saint Bernard fancier for life. Once you are owned by a Saint Bernard, it seems that no other breed will do. Perhaps it's his name, his origins, or his heritage that inspire this kind of devotion, but it is a fact.

Aside from being a wonderful companion dog, the Saint is also very much a guardian of his family and his home. His deep bark serves ample warning to all that one very large dog resides at this address.

The Saint is devoted to the children in his family and often takes hold of a child's hand, ever so gently, seeming to lead them where he thinks they should go. One impressive and true example of the Saint's devotion to children is the story of "Beggar," a Saint living in Sacramento, California, who was judged the 1962 "dog hero of the year." Beggar pulled three-year-old Bobby Mitchell out of the flooded American River, saving his life.

The 1970 "dog hero of the year" was another Saint Bernard—Polar Blu Samaritan von Barri, affectionately called "Grizzly Bear." This nickname proved pretty apropos, because Grizzly saved his mistress, Mrs. Theresa Gratias of Anchorage, Alaska, from a possible severe mauling when she inadvertently came between a real female grizzly bear and the bear's cub. The rescue instincts of a Saint's ancestors still remain in his soul.

A well-socialized Saint Bernard—a dog that has been through obedience school and accepted his master as his boss—is an exceptional pet. A Saint who has been shut away in the backyard, left in a kennel much of his life, and hasn't had much of life's experiences will be shy and difficult to manage. This is a breed that takes some effort on the part of master and family, but those efforts are rewarded with a companion par excellence.

If you provide your Saint with good care and the proper training, he will reward you by being a dependable and loyal companion. Mt. Chalet's Vanilla Fudge.

STANDARD for the Saint Bernard

Th he following is the American Kennel Club (AKC) standard for the Saint Bernard. Please refer to the standard of the governing kennel club in your country. **General**—Powerful, proportionately tall figure, strong and muscular in every part, with powerful head and most intelligent expression. In dogs with a dark mask the expression appears more stern, but never ill-natured.

Head—Like the whole body, very powerful and imposing. The massive skull is wide, slightly arched and the sides slope in a gentle curve into the very strongly developed, high cheek bones. Occiput only moderately developed. The supra-orbital ridge is very strongly developed and forms nearly a right angle with the long axis of the head. Deeply imbedded between the eyes and starting at the root of the muzzle, a furrow runs over the whole skull. It is strongly marked in the first half, gradually disappearing toward the base of the occiput. The lines at the sides of the head diverge considerably from the outer corner of the eyes toward the back of the head. The skin of the forehead, above the eyes, forms rather noticeable wrinkles, more or less pronounced, which converge toward the furrow. Especially when the dog is alert or at attention the wrinkles are more visible without in the least giving the impression of morosity. Too strongly developed wrinkles are not desired. The slope from the skull to the muzzle is sudden and rather steep.

The muzzle is short, does not taper, and the vertical depth at the root of the muzzle must be greater than the length of the muzzle. The bridge of the muzzle is not arched, but straight; in some dogs, occasionally, slightly broken. A rather wide, well-marked, shallow furrow runs from the root of the muzzle over the entire bridge of the muzzle to the nose. The flews of the upper jaw are strongly developed, not sharply cut, but turning in a beautiful curve into the lower edge, and slightly overhanging. The flews of the lower jaw must not be deeply pendant. The teeth should be sound and strong and should meet in either a scissors or an even bite; the scissors bite being preferable. The undershot bite, although sometimes found with good specimens, is not desirable. The overshot bite is a fault. A black roof to the mouth is desirable.

Nose (Schwamm)—Very substantial, broad, with wide open nostrils, and, like the lips, always black.

Ears—Of medium size, rather high set, with very strongly developed burr (Muschel) at the base. They stand slightly away from the head at the base, then drop with a sharp bend to the side and cling to the head without a turn. The flap is tender and forms a rounded triangle, slightly elongated toward the point, the front edge lying firmly to the head, whereas the back edge may stand somewhat away from the head, especially when the dog is at attention. Lightly set ears, which at the base immediately cling to the head, give it an oval and too little marked exterior, whereas a strongly developed base gives the skull a squarer, broader and much more expressive appearance.

According to the breed standard, a Saint Bernard's head should be very powerful and imposing. Ch. Rock Isle Heidi, owned by Betty-Anne Stenmark.

Ch. Heaven Hi's Silver and Gold, owned by Jerri Hobbs, has a good example of a lovely head with a nice, wide blaze and a dark mask over each eye.

Eyes—Set more to the front than the sides, are of medium size, dark brown, with intelligent, friendly expression, set moderately deep. The lower eyelids, as a rule, do not close completely and, if that is the case, form an angular wrinkle toward the inner corner of the eye. Eyelids which are too deeply pendant and show conspicuously the lachrymal glands, or a very red, thick haw, and eyes that are too light, are objectionable.

Neck—Set high, very strong and when alert or at attention is carried erect. Otherwise horizontally or slightly downward. The junction of head and neck is distinctly marked by an indentation. The nape of the neck is very muscular and rounded at the sides which makes the neck appear rather short. The dewlap of throat and neck is well pronounced: too strong development, however, is not desirable.

Shoulders—Sloping and broad, very muscular and powerful. The withers are strongly pronounced.

Chest—Very well arched, moderately deep, not reaching below the elbows.

Back—Very broad, perfectly straight as far as the haunches, from there gently sloping to the rump, and merging imperceptibly into the root of the tail.

Hindquarters—Well-developed. Legs very muscular.

Belly—Distinctly set off from the very powerful loin section, only little drawn up.

Tail—Starting broad and powerful directly from the rump is long, very heavy, ending in a powerful tip. In repose it hangs straight down, turning gently upward in the lower third only, which is not considered a fault. In a great many specimens the tail is carried with the end slightly bent and therefore hangs down in the shape of an *"f"*. In action all dogs carry the tail more or less turned upward. However it may not be carried too erect or by any means rolled over the back. A slight curling of the tip is sooner admissible.

The ideal Saint Bernard stands tall, is strong and muscular, and has an alert, intelligent expression.

Forearms—Very powerful and extraordinarily muscular.

Forelegs—Straight, strong.

Hind legs—Hocks of moderate angulation. Dewclaws are not desired; if present, they must not obstruct gait.

Feet—Broad, with strong toes, moderately closed, and with rather high knuckles. The so-called dewclaws which sometimes occur on the inside of the hind legs are imperfectly developed toes. They are of no use to the dog and are not taken into consideration in judging. They may be removed by surgery.

Coat—Very dense, short-haired (stockhaarig), lying smooth, tough, without however feeling rough to the touch. The thighs are slightly bushy. The tail at the root has longer and denser hair which gradually becomes shorter toward the tip. The tail appears bushy, not forming a flag.

Color—White with red or red with white, the red in its various shades; brindle patches with white markings. The colors red and brown-yellow are of entirely equal value. Necessary markings are: white chest, feet and tip of tail, noseband, collar or spot on the nape; the latter and blaze are very desirable. Never of one color or without white. Faulty are all other colors, except the favorite dark shadings on the head (mask) and ears. One distinguishes between mantle dogs and splash-coated dogs.

Although the Saint Bernard has an imposing physical appearance, he is one of the most gentle and affectionate breeds.

Height at Shoulder—Of the dog should be 27 $^1/_2$ inches minimum, of the bitch 25 $^1/_2$ inches. Female animals are of finer and more delicate build.

Considered as faults—are all deviations from the Standard, as for instance a swayback and a disproportionately long back, hocks too much bent, straight hindquarters, upward growing hair in spaces between the toes, out at elbows, cowhocks and weak pasterns.

LONGHAIRED

The longhaired type completely resembles the shorthaired type except for the coat which is not shorthaired (stockhaarig) but of medium length plain to slightly wavy, never rolled or curly and not shaggy either. Usually, on the back, especially from the region of the haunches to the rump, the hair is more wavy, a condition, by the way, that is slightly indicated in the shorthaired dogs. The tail is bushy with dense hair of moderate length. Rolled or curly hair, or a flag tail, is faulty. Face and ears are covered with short and soft hair; longer hair at the base of the ear is permissible. Forelegs only slightly feathered; thighs very bushy.

Approved April 13, 1998
Effective May 31, 1998

SELECTING the Right Saint Bernard for You

WHAT TO LOOK FOR IN A BREEDER

Once the prospective Saint owner satisfactorily answers all the questions relating to responsible ownership, he or she will undoubtedly want to rush out and purchase a puppy immediately. However, it is important not to be hasty with this decision. The purchase of any dog is an important step, because a well-cared-for dog will live for many years. Most Saint Bernards live eight to ten years, some longer. You will undoubtedly want the dog you live with for that length of time to be one you enjoy.

It is extremely important in this breed that your Saint is purchased from a breeder who has earned a reputation over

Purchase your Saint puppy from a breeder who has a reputation for producing mentally and physically sound dogs.

the years for consistently producing dogs that are mentally and physically sound. Not only is a sound and stable temperament of paramount importance in a large breed of this kind, but there are also a number of diseases that exist in the breed which good breeders are concerned about. Unfortunately, the buyer must indeed beware in that there are always those who are ready and willing to exploit a breed for financial gain with no thought given to its health or welfare, or to the homes in which the dogs will be living.

The only way a breeder can earn a reputation for producing quality animals is through a well-thought-out breeding program in which rigid selectivity is imposed. Selective breeding is aimed at maintaining the virtues of a breed and eliminating genetic weaknesses. This process is time-consuming and costly. Therefore, responsible Saint breeders protect their

A responsible breeder will take the necessary steps to make sure that his or her puppies are well-socialized before they go to their new homes.

investment by providing the utmost in prenatal care for their brood matrons, and maximum care and nutrition for the resulting offspring. Once the puppies arrive, the knowledgeable breeder makes sure they are well socialized before they go to their new homes.

The governing kennel clubs in the different countries of the world maintain lists of local breed clubs and breeders that can lead a prospective dog buyer to responsible breeders of quality stock. If you are not be sure of where to contact a respected breeder in your area, we strongly recommend contacting your local kennel club for recommendations.

The buyer should look for cleanliness in both the dogs and the areas in which the dogs are kept. Cleanliness is the first clue that tells you how much the breeder cares about the dogs he or she owns.

It is extremely important that the buyer knows the character and quality of a puppy's parents. Good temperament and good health are inherited, and if the puppy's parents are not sound in these respects there is not much likelihood that they will produce offspring that are. Never buy a Saint from anyone who has no knowledge of the puppy's parents or the kind of care a puppy has been given from birth to the time you see him.

HEALTH CONCERNS

There is every possibility that you can find a reputable breeder in your area who will not only be able to provide the right Saint for you but also will have both of the puppy's parents on the premises. This gives you an opportunity to see firsthand what kind of dogs are in the background of the puppy you are considering. Good breeders are always willing to have you see their dogs and to inspect the facility in which the dogs are raised. These breeders will also be able to discuss with you problems that exist in the breed and how they deal with these problems.

Heart Disease

Just as in humans, various forms of heart disease affect Saint Bernards. Since heart disease is known to run in families, good questions for the breeder are, "How long does your line of Saints normally live?" and "Have you ever known any heart disease to exist in your line?"

Hip Dysplasia

Simply put, hip dysplasia is a failure of the head of the femur to fit snugly into the acetabulum, with resulting degrees of lameness and faulty movement. The inheritance of the defect is polygenic, which means there is no simple answer to the elimination of the problem. Breeders routinely perform x-rays on their breeding stock and breed only from superior animals who have been graded in the categories deemed acceptable for breeding. While it is important that both the sire and dam have been examined and cleared for breeding, it is just as important that the parents' littermates, grandparents, the grandparents' littermates, and so on, have been cleared.

Family selection is at least as important as individual selection in the case of polygenic diseases. The hip status of the parents of the litter and the incidence of hip dysplasia in the breeder's line would be an important question to ask any breeder of Saint Bernards. As a pet owner, it is important for you to know that individual dogs whose hips might not rate above a "fair" grade can lead a long and normal life.

Osteosarcoma

Bone cancer is not uncommon in the Saint Bernard, and as we now know from human medicine, tendencies toward certain types of cancer are more prevalent in some families than others. Osteosarcoma manifests itself in the Saint by persistent lameness of a leg, and a malignant tumor will develop. Ask the Saint breeder, "Have you had occurrences of osteosarcoma, or any other cancers, in your line?"

Try to see the sire and the dam of the puppy that you are considering. This will give you a better idea of what your puppy will grow up to look and act like.

Bloat

Otherwise known as acute gastric dilation-torsion, it can rapidly kill a dog with no prior history of problems. Large, deep-chested dogs are most affected. Prior to bloating, canine victims typically eat a big meal, drink large quantities of water, and exercise within two or three hours after eating. Their stomachs fill with gas and/or fluids and become severely distended and may twist. Left untreated, death can occur in just a few hours. Some lines seem to be more affected by this condition than others. Fortunately, better management of nutrition and exercise has led to fewer fatal cases of this disease.

Entropion

There are four common abnormalities of the eyelids, and entropion is the one most often seen in the Saint Bernard. This is a condition in which the eyelid turns in (usually the lower lid), and it affects breeds with loose skin on the head. Entropion is a hereditary defect, so affected dogs and their close relatives should not be used for breeding. Entropion is noticeable even to the novice pet owner, because most affected dogs will not open their eyes fully and seem to squint. The eye orifice is mucky with a yellow discharge, and the haws are abnormally red.

QUESTIONS AND ANSWERS

A discussion of the diseases that can affect the Saint is not to imply that all Saint lines are afflicted with them. However, the responsible breeder will always be more than happy to discuss his or her experience, if any, with the problems.

All breeds of dog have genetic problems that must be addressed, and just because a male and female do not develop problems, this does not mean that their pedigrees are free of something that could be entirely incapacitating. Again, rely upon recommendations or information from national kennel clubs or local breed clubs when looking for a breeder.

A healthy dog is a happy dog. The breeder from which you obtain your puppy should provide you with a copy of the dog's medical history.

Do not be surprised if a concerned breeder asks many questions about you and the environment in which your Saint will be raised. Good breeders are just as concerned with the quality of the homes to which their dogs are going as you, the buyer are about obtaining a sound and healthy dog.

Do not think a good Saint puppy can only come from a large kennel. On the contrary, many of the best breeders today raise dogs in their homes as a hobby. It is important, however, that you not allow yourself to fall into the hands of an irresponsible "backyard breeder." Backyard breeders separate themselves from the hobby breeder by their total lack of regard for the health of their breeding stock. They do not test their stock for genetic problems, nor are they concerned with how or where their puppies are raised.

We offer one important bit of advice to the prospective Saint buyer. If the person is attempting to sell you a puppy with no questions asked—go elsewhere.

RECOGNIZING A HEALTHY PUPPY

Most Saint breeders in the US do not release their puppies until the puppies have been given their "puppy shots." Normally, this is at about seven or eight weeks of age. At this age, the puppies will bond extremely well with their new owners and they are entirely weaned. Nursing puppies

Puppies that are still nursing receive temporary immunization from their mother.

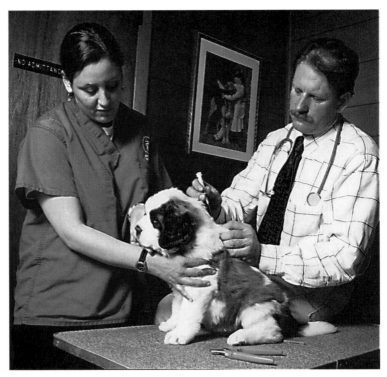

A puppy is very vulnerable to outside diseases. Make sure that your Saint puppy receives all his necessary inoculations before he socializes with other dogs. receive temporary immunization from their mother. Once weaned, however, a puppy is highly susceptible to many infectious diseases that can be transmitted via the hands and clothing of people. Therefore, it behooves you to make sure your puppy is fully inoculated before he leaves his home environment and to know when any additional inoculations should be given.

Above all, the Saint puppy you buy should be happy, outgoing and self-confident. The Saint's protective instinct develops in adulthood. A shy or suspicious puppy is definitely a poor choice, as is a shy, shrinking violet puppy or one that appears sick and listless. Selecting a puppy of that sort because you feel sorry for him will undoubtedly lead to heartache and difficulty, to say nothing of the veterinary costs that you may incur in getting the puppy well.

If at all possible, take the puppy you are interested in away from his littermates into another room or another part of the kennel. The smells will remain the same for the puppy so he should still feel secure and maintain his outgoing personality, but it will give you an opportunity to inspect the puppy more closely. A healthy little Saint puppy will be strong and sturdy to the touch, never bony or obese and bloated. The inside of the puppy's ears should be pink and clean. Dark discharge or a bad odor could indicate ear mites, a sure sign of poor maintenance. The healthy Saint puppy's breath smells sweet—well, maybe not exactly sweet, but it should have that unique smell dog breeders lovingly call "puppy breath." The teeth are clean and white, and there should never be any malformation of the mouth or jaw. The puppy's eyes should be clear and bright and have a soft, almost wise look, which is typical of a Saint baby. Eyes that appear runny and irritated indicate serious problems.

There should be no sign of discharge from the nose, nor should it be crusted or runny. Coughing or diarrhea are danger signals, as are any eruptions on the skin. The coat should be soft and lustrous.

The healthy Saint puppy's front legs should be straight as posts, strong and true. Even these giant breed puppies will appear active, agile and strong, although they may stumble over their own feet occasionally. Do not mistake this for unsoundness, but if you have any doubts, discuss them with the breeder.

Male or Female?

While both the male and the female are capable of becoming excellent companions and are equally easy to train, do consider the fact that a male Saint will be larger (sometimes 30 or 40 pounds heavier) than his sister and will have all the muscle power to go with the extra weight. Give serious consideration to your own strength and stature.

There are other sex-related differences to consider. While the Saint Bernard is a clean breed and easy to housebreak, the male of any breed of dog has a natural instinct to lift his leg and "mark" his territory. Thankfully, one of the virtues of the Saint Bernard is that unlike a macho Chihuahua or terrier, the male Saint is much less likely to "mark" the inside of your home.

Females, on the other hand, have their own set of problems. Females' semiannual heat cycles commence at about six months of age. During these heat cycles lasting approximately 21 days, the female must be confined to avoid soiling her surroundings with the bloody discharge that accompanies estrus. Like everything else about the Saint Bernard, the bloody discharge is much more of a problem compared with smaller breeds in which the discharge is usually referred to as "spotting." There are "britches" sold at pet shops that assist in keeping the female in heat from soiling the house. She must also be watched carefully to prevent males from gaining access to her, or she will become pregnant. Do not expect the marauding male to be deterred by the britches if your female has them on.

Despite sex-related differences, both male and female Saints make equally wonderful companions.

Both of these sex-related problems can be avoided by having the pet Saint altered. Spaying the female and neutering the male saves the pet owner all the headaches of either of the sex-related problems without changing the character of your Saint. If altering a dog changes him or her at all, it is merely to make the dog an even more amiable companion. Above all, altering your pet precludes the possibility that he'll add to the serious worldwide pet overpopulation problems.

SELECTING A SHOW-PROSPECT PUPPY

If you are considering a show career for your puppy, all the foregoing information regarding soundness and health applies. It must be remembered though, that spaying and neutering are not reversible procedures and, once done, eliminate the possibility of ever breeding or showing your Saint in conformation shows in the US. (Altered dogs may, however, be shown in obedience trials and many other competitive events.)

There are a good number of additional points to be considered for the show dog. First of all, the most any breeder can offer is an opinion on the "show potential" of a particular puppy. The most promising eight-week-old Saint puppy can grow up to be just an average adult. A breeder has no control over this. It is sometimes said that an unknowing new owner can ruin a "show prospect" in about three weeks with improper feeding and exercise, and this certainly holds true with a giant breed puppy like the Saint.

Any predictions breeders make about a puppy's future are based on their experience with past litters that have produced winning show dogs. It is obvious that the more successful a breeder has been in producing winning Saints over the years, the broader his or her base of comparison will be.

A puppy's potential as a show dog is determined by how closely he adheres to the demands of the standard of the breed. While most breeders concur that there is no such thing as "a sure thing" when it comes to predicting winners, they are also quick to agree that the older a puppy is, the better your chances are of making any predictions. Evaluating the puppies and grading a litter is best done at eight weeks of age.

It makes little difference to the owner of a pet if their Saint is a little high in the rear or if he carries his tail up over his back. These faults do not interfere with a Saint becoming a healthy, loving companion. However, these flaws would keep that Saint from a top-winning show career.

While it certainly behooves the prospective buyer of a show prospect puppy to be as familiar with the standard of the breed as possible, it is even more important for the buyer to put his or herself into the hands of a successful and respected breeder of winning Saints. The experienced breeder knows that there are certain age-related shortcomings in young Saints that maturity will take care of and that there are other faults that completely eliminate the puppy from consideration as a show prospect.

Breeders are always looking for the right homes in which to place their show-prospect puppies. They can be particularly helpful when they know you plan to show one of their dogs. The important thing to remember in choosing your first show prospect is that cuteness may not be consistent with quality. While showmanship and a charismatic personality are critical to a show dog's success in the ring, those qualities are the frosting on the cake, so to speak. They are the characteristics that put the well-made Saint over the top.

An extroverted or particularly loving puppy in the litter might decide he belongs to you. If you are simply looking for a pet, then he is the puppy for you. However, if you are genuinely interested in showing your Saint, you must keep your head and, without disregarding good temperament, give serious consideration to what the standard says a show-type Saint Bernard must be.

The complete standard of the breed is presented in this book, and there are also a number of other books that can assist the newcomer in learning more about the breed.

If you are considering a show career for your Saint, be certain that he is sound and healthy. Ch. Opdyke's Hair, owned by Marcia Carter, winning the Veteran Dog Class under the author at the 1980 S.B.C.A. National Specialty.

PUPPY OR ADULT?

A puppy is not your only option when contemplating the purchase of a Saint. In

some cases, an adult dog may be just the answer. It certainly eliminates the trials and tribulations of housebreaking, chewing, and the myriad of other problems associated with a young puppy.

On occasion, adult Saints are available from homes or kennels breeding show dogs. Their breeders realize the older dog would be far happier in a family situation where he can watch television, take hikes, and be a part of a family instead of living out his life in a kennel run.

Puppies are like babies— they require constant attention. Whether you choose a puppy or an adult Saint, you will gain a loving and gentle canine friend.

Adult Saints can adjust to their new homes with relative ease. Most new owners are amazed at how quickly it all happens and how quickly these adults become devoted to their new families. After all, a Saint lives to have his own person or family, and even those raised in a kennel seem to blossom in the home environment.

When the proper arrangements have been made, an adult Saint that has been given kind and loving care in his previous home could be the perfect answer for an elderly person or someone who is away from home during the day. While it would be unreasonable to expect a young puppy not to relieve himself in the house if you are gone for more than just a few hours, it would be surprising to find a housebroken Saint who, in adulthood, would even consider relieving himself in his home.

A few adult Saints may have become set in their ways, and while you may not have to contend with the problems of puppyhood, do realize that the rare adult might have developed habits that do not entirely suit you or your lifestyle. Arrange to bring an adult Saint into your home on a trial basis. That way, neither you nor the dog will be obligated if either of you decide you are incompatible.

IDENTIFICATION PAPERS

The purchase of any purebred dog entitles you to three very important documents: a health record containing an inoculation list, a copy of the dog's pedigree, and the registration certificate.

Your Saint's medical history is vital to his future health. Obtain a copy of your puppy's health records from your breeder.

Health Record

Most Saint breeders have initiated the necessary inoculation series for their puppies by the time the puppies are seven weeks of age. These inoculations protect the puppies against distemper, hepatitis, leptospirosis, and canine parvovirus. Depending on where the breeder is located, puppies may also be vaccinated against coronavirus and Lyme disease. In most cases, rabies inoculations are not given until a puppy is four months of age or older.

There is a set series of inoculations developed to combat these infectious diseases, and it is extremely important that you obtain a record of the shots your puppy has been given and the dates the shots were administered. This way, the veterinarian you choose will be able to continue on with the appropriate inoculation series as needed.

Pedigree

The pedigree is your dog's "family tree." The breeder must supply you with a copy of this document, authenticating your puppy's ancestors back to at least the third generation. All purebred dogs have a pedigree. The pedigree does not imply that a dog is of show quality. It is simply a chronological list of ancestors.

Registration Certificate

The registration certificate is the canine world's "birth certificate." This certificate is issued by a country's governing kennel club. When you transfer the ownership of your Saint from the breeder's name to your own name, the transaction is entered on this certificate. Once it is mailed to the kennel club, it is permanently recorded in their computerized files.

Your breeder should have started your puppy on a nutritious diet. Stick to this original plan for as long as possible, so as not to cause any stomach upset.

Keep all these documents in a safe place, because you will need them when you visit your veterinarian or if you ever wish to breed or show your Saint.

DIET SHEET

Your Saint is the happy, healthy puppy he is because the breeder has been carefully feeding and caring for him. Every breeder has her own particular way of doing this. Most breeders give the new owner a written record that details the amount and kind of food a puppy has been receiving. Follow these recommendations to the letter, at least for the first month or two after the puppy comes to live with you.

The diet sheet should indicate the number of times a day your puppy has been accustomed to being fed and the kind of vitamin supplementation, if any, he has been receiving. Following the prescribed procedure will reduce the chance of upset stomach and loose stools.

Usually, a breeder's diet sheet projects the increases and changes in food that will be necessary as your puppy grows from week to week. If the sheet does not include this information, ask the breeder for suggestions regarding increases and the eventual changeover to adult food.

In the unlikely event you are not supplied with a diet sheet by the breeder and are unable to get one, your veterinarian will be able to advise you in this respect. There are countless foods now being manufactured expressly to meet the nutritional needs of puppies and growing dogs. A trip down the pet aisle at your local pet supply store will prove just how many choices you have. Two important tips to remember: Read labels carefully for content, and purchase food from established, reliable manufacturers, because you are more likely to get what you pay for.

To avoid unnecessary complications, you should have your Saint checked by a veterinarian 24 hours from the time you take him home.

HEALTH GUARANTEE

Any reputable breeder will be more than willing to supply a written agreement that the sale of your Saint is contingent upon the puppy passing a veterinarian's examination. Ideally, you will be able to arrange an appointment with your chosen veterinarian right after you have picked up your puppy from the breeder and before you take the puppy home. If this is not possible, you should not delay this procedure any longer than 24 hours from the time you take your puppy home.

TEMPERAMENT AND SOCIALIZATION

Temperament is both hereditary and learned. An inherited good temperament can be ruined by poor treatment and lack of proper socialization. A Saint puppy that has inherited bad temperament is a poor risk as a companion or as a show dog and should certainly never be bred. In fact, a Saint Bernard

Having a pet is a lifelong commitment. Choose your puppy carefully to ensure a long and lasting relationship.

with poor temperament is a dangerous weapon and not suitable to be kept as a pet. Therefore, it is critical that you obtain a happy puppy from a breeder who is determined to produce good temperaments and has taken all the necessary steps to provide the proper socialization.

Temperaments in the same litter can range from strong-willed and outgoing on the high end of the scale to reserved and retiring at the low end. A puppy that is so bold and strong-willed as to be foolhardy and uncontrollable could easily be a difficult adult that needs a very firm hand. In a breed as large and strong as a Saint, this would hardly be a dog for the owner who is mild and reserved in demeanor or frail in physique. In every human-canine relationship there must be a pack leader and a follower. In order to achieve his full potential, the Saint must have an owner who remains in charge at all times. The Saint himself wants and needs this kind of relationship.

It is important to remember that a Saint puppy may be as happy as a clam living at home with you and your family, but if the socialization begun by the breeder is not continued, that sunny disposition will not extend outside your front door. From the day the young Saint arrives at your home, you must be committed to helping him meet and coexist with all human beings and animals. Do not worry about the Saint's protective instinct—this comes with maturity. Never encourage aggressive behavior on the part of your puppy or give him a reason to fear strangers.

If you are fortunate enough to have children who are well past the toddler stage either in the household or living nearby, your socialization task will be assisted considerably. Saints raised with children seem to have a distinct advantage in socialization. Be aware that children must be supervised and taught to treat the puppy properly.

Saints are apt to "adopt" the household's children and make raising the children their own special project. Children and Saint puppies seem to understand each other, and in some way known only to the puppies and children themselves, they give each other the confidence to face the trying ordeal of growing up.

The children in your own household are not the only children your puppy should spend time with. The more, the merrier! Every child and adult who enters your household should be asked to pet your puppy.

Your puppy should go everywhere with you: to the post office, the market, the shopping mall—wherever. Be prepared to create a stir wherever you go. The public seems to hold a special admiration for the Saint, and while they might not want to approach a mature dog, most people are quite taken with the Saint baby and will undoubtedly want to pet your youngster. There is nothing in the world that is better for the puppy.

If your puppy backs off from a stranger, give the person a treat to offer your puppy. You must insist that your young Saint be comfortable with any strangers you approve of, regardless of sex, age, or race. It is not up to your puppy to decide who he will or will not tolerate.

If your Saint has a show career in his future, there are other things (in addition to just being handled) that he will have to be taught. All show dogs must learn to have their mouths opened and inspected by the judge. The judge must be able to check the teeth. Males must be accustomed to having their testicles touched, because the dog show judge must determine that all male dogs are "complete," meaning that there are two normal-sized testicles in the scrotum. These inspections must begin in puppyhood and be done on a regular basis.

All Saints must learn to get along with other dogs as well as humans. If you are fortunate enough to have a "puppy preschool" or dog training class nearby, attend with as much regularity as you can. A young Saint that has been exposed regularly to other dogs from puppyhood will learn to adapt and accept other dogs and other breeds much more readily than one that seldom sees strange dogs.

Two-year-old Katelynn Crofford enjoys smooching with Celestial Saints Cinderella, owned by Tina McIllveene Crofford.

These baby Saints will grow into massive adult dogs. Be prepared for the changes in size and behavior as your puppy matures.

THE ADOLESCENT SAINT BERNARD

You will be amazed how quickly the youngster you first brought home begins to develop into a full-grown Saint Bernard. Some breeding lines shoot up to full size very rapidly, while others mature more slowly. At about six months of age, most Saint puppies become lanky and ungainly, growing in and out of proportion seemingly from one day to the next—not surprising, because the average Saint Bernard puppy grows to between 80 and 100 pounds in the first six months of his life.

Somewhere between 12 and 18 months, your Saint will have attained his full height. However, body and muscle development continues on until three years of age in some lines and up to four or more in others.

Many Saint owners have been asked, "How much does your dog eat?" The answer is, not nearly as much as one might think. Giant breeds don't eat much more than the average large breed, such as a Rhodesian Ridgeback or an Alaskan Malamute.

Food needs increase during this growth period, and the average Saint seems as if he can never get enough to eat. There are some puppies, however, that go through a very finicky stage and seem to eat only enough to keep from starving. Saint puppies are as individualistic as human children.

The amount of food you give your Saint should be adjusted to how much he will readily consume at each meal. If the entire meal is eaten quickly, add a small amount to the next feeding and continue to do so as the need increases. This method will ensure that you give your puppy enough food. You must also pay close attention to the dog's appearance and condition, because you do not want a puppy to become overweight or obese.

At eight weeks of age, a Saint puppy is eating three meals a day. By the time he is three months old, the puppy can do well on two meals a day, perhaps with a snack in the middle of the day. If your puppy does not eat the food offered, he is either not hungry or not well. Your dog will eat when he is hungry. If you suspect the dog is not well, a trip to the veterinarian is in order.

This adolescent period is a particularly important one, because it is the time your Saint must learn all the household and social rules by which he will live for the rest of his life. Your patience and commitment during this time will not only produce an obedient canine but will forge a bond between the two of you that will grow and ripen into a wonderful relationship.

As puppies mature, their nutritional needs change. An eight-week-old puppy needs three meals a day; by the time he is three months of age, two meals are sufficient.

CARING for Your Saint Bernard

FEEDING AND NUTRITION

Following the diet sheet provided by your puppy's breeder is the best way to make sure your Saint Bernard is obtaining the right amount and the correct type of food for his age. Do your best not to change the puppy's diet and you will be far less apt to run into digestive problems and diarrhea. Diarrhea is very serious in young puppies. Puppies with diarrhea can dehydrate very rapidly, causing severe problems and even death.

If it is necessary to change your puppy's diet for any reason, this should never be done abruptly. Begin by adding a quarter-cup of the new food and reduce the old product by the same amount. Gradually increase the amount of the new food over a week or ten days until the meal consists entirely of the new product. A puppy's digestive system is extremely delicate. Any changes you make in what the puppy eats should be done carefully and slowly.

Providing your Saint with a well-balanced and nutritious diet will keep him in excellent condition. Ch. Flofairs Almost A Ten, owned by R.F. and N.M. Demory.

The total amount of food you give your Saint puppy should also be adjusted carefully. Give the puppy all he will eat within 10 or 15 minutes of the time you put the food dish down. Take the dish up after that amount of time has elapsed. If the puppy consumes the entire meal, add a small amount to the next meal, balancing what you add with what the puppy will eat.

There is the occasional Saint puppy that is a true glutton, and he will eat more than he needs to stay healthy. One rule of thumb is that you should be able to feel the ribs and backbone with just a slight layer of fat and muscle over them. The puppy should be firm to the touch and not sloppy, with rolls of loose flesh.

Considering what we now know about deep-chested breeds, such as the Saint, and their predisposition to bloat and torsion, large meals should be avoided. It is better to feed

smaller meals two or even three times daily, instead of one large meal, or to make dry food available at all times. This is sometimes called "free feeding." Also recommended is a high-fat diet, which allows the stomach to empty more slowly after meals. When mixing the dog's meal, add water to the dry food first and let the dry food get soggy so the dog's stomach feels full faster and he won't drink as much. Never exercise your Saint immediately after eating, and always restrict his water intake for a short time afterwards.

"Balanced" Diets

In the US, dog foods must meet standards set by the Subcommittee on Canine Nutrition of the National Research Council in order to qualify as "complete and balanced." As proof of compliance, dog food manufacturers list the ingredients of their product on every box, bag, or can. The ingredients are listed by weight in descending order.

Feed your puppy a balanced diet containing the essential nutrients that he needs to grow into a healthy adult.

To achieve optimum health and condition, make sure your Saint has a constant supply of fresh clean water and a balanced diet containing the essential nutrients in correct proportions. This can be achieved with a good quality kibble to which a small amount of canned, fresh, or cooked meat may be added. Pet stores and supermarkets carry a wide selection of foods manufactured by respected firms. An important thing to remember in selecting a dog food is that all dogs are meat-eating animals. Animal protein and fats are essential to the well-being of any breed of dog.

The main ingredient in any commercially prepared food you buy should be animal protein. The remaining ingredients in quality products will provide the carbohydrates, fats, roughage, and minerals your dog needs.

Puppies need a lot of attention. If you have a question regarding your Saint's health, check with your vet.

Do not feed your Saint products that contain sugar. Excessive amounts of sugar can lead to severe dental problems and unwanted weight gain.

Oversupplementation

A great deal of controversy exists today regarding the orthopedic problems that exist in dogs, such as hip, elbow, and patella (knee) dysplasia. Some claim these problems and a wide variety of chronic skin conditions are entirely hereditary. Others feel that they are a result, in whole or in part, of overuse of mineral and vitamin supplements in puppies and young dogs.

Never exceed the prescribed amount of vitamins. Some breeders insist that all recommended dosages should be cut in half when supplements are used with the heavily fortified commercial foods available today.

There may be special periods in a Saint's life when vitamin supplementation is necessary: rapid growth in puppyhood, pregnancy, and nursing are high-stress periods, and your veterinarian may suggest vitamin supplementation.

Never feed your Saint from the table while you are eating. Dogs can very quickly become addicted to the exotic smells of the foods you eat and turn up their nose at the less-tempting, but probably far more nutritious, food in their regular meals.

Dogs do not care if food looks like a hot dog or a wedge of cheese. They only care about the food's smell and taste. Products manufactured to look like other foods are designed to appeal to the humans who buy them. These foods often contain high amounts of preservatives, sugars, and dyes, none of which are suitable for your dog.

Special Diets

There are now any number of commercially prepared diets for dogs with special dietary needs. The overweight, underweight, or geriatric dog can have his nutritional needs met, as can puppies and growing dogs. The calorie content of these foods is adjusted accordingly.

Common sense must prevail. What is true for humans is true for dogs—too many calories and too little exercise will increase weight. Increasing exercise and reducing calorie counts will bring weight down.

Occasionally, an adolescent Saint will become a problem eater. Trying to tempt the dog to eat by handfeeding him or offering him special foods only serves to make the problem worse. Your dog will quickly learn to play the waiting game, fully aware that those special things he likes will be presented to him sooner than later. Feed your Saint the proper food you want him to eat. The dog may turn up his nose for a day or two and refuse to eat anything. However, you can rest assured that when your dog is really hungry, he will eat.

A healthy dog will not starve himself to death. He may not eat enough to keep himself in the shape we find ideal and attractive, but he will definitely eat enough to maintain himself. If your Saint is not eating properly and appears to be thin and listless, it is probably best to consult your veterinarian.

BATHING AND GROOMING

The breeder from whom you purchased your Saint will probably have begun to accustom the puppy to grooming just as soon as he was old enough to stand. You must continue with grooming sessions or begin them at once if for some reason they have not been started. It is imperative that you both learn to cooperate in this endeavor in order to make it an easy and pleasant experience.

Brushing your Saint's coat is a good way to detect any skin irritations. It also helps keep the coat clean and lustrous.

Your Saint will not require much grooming time or

equipment. That is not to say that he needs no grooming at all. Regular brushing keeps the coat clean, odor-free, and healthy.

Regular grooming gives you the opportunity to keep on top of your dog's home health care needs. If you find your dog is licking himself and causing a skin irritation, try applying a commercially available foul-tasting but non-toxic liquid that will not harm the dog in any way. Such things as trimming nails, cleaning ears, and checking teeth can be attended to at this time as well.

Brush the hair vigorously using a good slicker brush. Follow the brushing with a comb, being sure to comb through the dense undercoat right to the skin. A fine spray of coat dressing and a quick rub with a towel or washcloth will give your Saint's coat a real glow.

It's important that your Saint remains still while on the grooming table to avoid any mishaps. Be very careful not to cut into the quick when trimming your Saint's nails.

This is a good time to accustom your Saint to having his nails trimmed and his feet inspected. Always inspect your dog's feet for cracked pads. Check between the toes for splinters and thorns, paying particular attention to any swollen or tender areas.

We suggest attending to your dog's nails at least every other week. Long nails on a Saint are not only unattractive, they spread and weaken the foot. The nails of a Saint that isn't exercising outdoors on rough terrain will grow long very quickly. Do not allow the nails to become overgrown and then expect to cut them back easily. Each nail has a blood vessel running through the center that is called the "quick." The quick grows close to the end of the nail and contains very sensitive nerve endings. If the nail is allowed to grow too long, it will be impossible to cut it back to a proper length without cutting into the quick. This causes severe pain to the dog and can also result in a great deal of bleeding that may be very difficult to stop.

Nails can be trimmed with canine nail clippers or with an electric nail grinder (also called a drummel). We prefer using the latter with the fine grinding disc, because this

allows you to trim back the nail a little bit at a time, practically eliminating any bleeding. Some Saints have white nails in which you can easily visualize the quick, but others have dark nails, making it practically impossible to see where the quick ends. Regardless of which nail-trimming device you use, you must proceed with caution and remove only a small portion of the nail at a time.

If the quick is nipped in the trimming process, there are a number of blood-clotting products available at pet shops that will almost immediately stem the flow of blood. It is wise to have one of these products on hand in case your dog breaks a nail in some way.

Saints look much better with their whiskers trimmed. This can be done with a good pair of blunt-tip barber sheers. The rounded tips preclude the possibility of your Saint injuring his eye by making a sudden move.

Regular brushing practically eliminates the need to give your Saint a wet bath. If your dog gets into a foul-smelling substance of some kind, there are many "dry bath" products that can be used to both clean the coat and eliminate odor.

Care should always be given to the state of your dog's teeth. If your dog has been accustomed to chewing hard dog biscuits or gnawing on large rawhide bones or any of the wide variety of Nylabone® products since puppyhood, it is unlikely that you will have any dental problems. This chewing activity assists greatly in removing dental plaque, which is the major cause of tooth decay. Any sign of redness of the gums or tooth decay merits expert attention.

EXERCISE

The Saint that is given plenty of opportunity to exercise is a much happier and healthier dog. Any dog that expends his energy in physical activity is far less apt to become mischievous and destructive in the home.

Needless to say, puppies should never be forced to exercise. Young Saint Bernards need the opportunity to exercise at will and may enjoy a walk on lead or a romp through the park or on the local beach. However, until the dog is mature (and only then if he is properly conditioned, like a young human athlete), he should not be exposed to more arduous and lengthy exercise.

Many Saint owners who condition their dogs for the show ring will exercise them using the Springer bicycle attachment on a bike. It is important, however, to use good judgment in any exercise program. Begin slowly and increase the distance to be covered very gradually over an extended period of time. Obviously, this type of exercise should never be undertaken during hot weather or after eating.

SOCIALIZATION

A young Saint that has never been exposed to strangers, traffic noises, or boisterous children could become confused and frightened. It is important that a Saint owner give his or her dog the opportunity to experience all of these situations gradually and with his trusted owner present for support.

Saint puppies are usually friendly and more than happy to accept strangers, but as they mature, their attitudes can change. They can become reserved and suspicious if the socialization process is neglected. It is absolutely imperative that you continue the socialization process and maintain the pack leader role with your Saint as he matures.

Exercise gives your Saint the chance to work off excess energy or stress, as well as the opportunity to stay physically fit.

A well-trained Saint can serve both as a guard dog and as a good citizen. The dog knows that he should obey your commands under all circumstances, that "no!" means just that, and that once you give that command he must stop whatever he is doing.

HOUSEBREAKING and Training Your Saint Bernard

There is no breed of dog that cannot be trained. Granted, there are some dogs that provide a real challenge to this statement, but in most cases this has more to do with the trainer and his or her training methods than with the dog's inability to learn. Using the proper approach, any dog that is not mentally deficient can be taught to be a good canine citizen. Many dog owners do not understand how a dog learns, nor do they realize they can be breed-specific in their approach to training.

A Saint Bernard is as smart as his owner allows him to be. It's amazing how quickly puppies can learn. This capacity is greater than most humans realize. It is important to remember, though, that young puppies also forget with great speed unless they are reminded of what they have learned through continual reinforcement.

Saint Bernards have a great capacity to learn new things. Conducting short and fun lessons will keep them interested and eager to learn.

As puppies leave the nest, they begin their search for two things: a pack leader and rules, set down by that leader, by which they can abide. Dog owners often fail miserably in supplying these very basic needs. Instead, the owner immediately begins to respond to the demands of the puppy—and puppies can quickly learn to be very demanding. In the case of little dogs, this can be a nuisance. In the case of giant dogs like the Saint, this can produce aggression, an uncontrollable danger to society.

A puppy quickly learns that he will be allowed into the house when he whines, instead of learning that he can only enter the house when he is not whining. Instead of learning that the only way he will be fed is to follow a set procedure (i.e., sitting or lying down on command), the poorly educated Saint puppy learns that leaping about the kitchen and creating a stir is what gets results.

If your Saint finds that a growl or a snap permits him to have his own way, rest assured that this behavior will continue. In

fact, it will only increase. On the other hand, if a challenge on the dog's part is met with stern, uncompromising correction, the dog knows that the behavior does not evoke the desired response.

If the young puppy does not see his owner as pack leader, the puppy assumes the role of pack leader. If there are no rules imposed, the puppy learns to make his own rules. Unfortunately, the negligent owner continually reinforces the puppy's decisions by allowing him to govern the household.

The key to successful training lies in establishing the proper relationship between dog and owner. The owner or the owning family must be the pack leader, and the individual or family must provide the rules by which the dog abides.

The Saint is easily trained to almost any task. It is important to remember, however, that the breed does not respond to or require violent treatment. Positive reinforcement is the key to successfully training a Saint Bernard and will produce a happy, confident companion.

A Saint puppy should always be a winner. With the aid of a toy or tidbit, begin teaching simple lessons like the "come" command when the puppy is already on his way to you. Do not expect the young puppy to come dashing over to you when he is engrossed in some wonderful adventure. The puppy quickly learns that he will be praised for coming on command, which is better than associating the word with his owner's anger because he did not respond to the word "come."

Housebreaking Made Easy

The best method of housebreaking is to avoid accidents happening. Our motto is, "Puppies don't make mistakes, people do." The young puppy has no idea what housebreaking means, and therefore he can hardly be accused of breaking a rule. You must teach the puppy what a fine little tyke he is by attending to his needs outdoors. Fortunately, the Saint Bernard is very easily housetrained— which is a good thing, considering that a mistake from even an eight-week-old Saint puppy looks more like Lake Superior than a puddle. This is not a breed for which paper-training is an option, because it would take the *New York Times* Sunday edition to soak up just one puddle.

We take a puppy outdoors to relieve himself after every meal, after every nap, and after every 15 or 20 minutes of playtime. We carry the puppy outdoors to avoid the opportunity of an accident occurring on the way. Obviously, you are not going to carry your Saint puppy for very long, but experience has shown that most Saint puppies are completely housebroken by about 12 weeks of age.

Housebreaking is a much easier task with the use of a crate. Most breeders use the fiberglass-type crates approved by the airlines for shipping live animals. They are easy to clean and can be used for the entire life of the dog.

Take your puppy outside to relieve himself after every nap, after every meal, and after 15 or 20 minutes of playtime.

Some first-time dog owners may see the crate method of housebreaking as cruel. What they do not understand is that all dogs need a place of their own to retreat to. A puppy will soon look to his crate as his own private den. Use of a crate reduces housetraining time down to an absolute minimum.

Begin by feeding your Saint puppy in the crate. Keep the door closed and latched while the puppy is eating. When the meal is finished, open the cage and carry the puppy outdoors to the spot where you want him to learn to eliminate. If you consistently take your puppy to the same spot, you will reinforce the habit of going there for that purpose.

It is important that you do not let the puppy loose after eating without first making sure he has been outside to do his business. Young puppies will eliminate almost immediately after eating or drinking. They will also be ready to relieve themselves when they first wake up and after playing. If you keep a watchful eye on your puppy, you will quickly learn when this is about to take place. A puppy usually circles and sniffs the floor just before he relieves himself.

Do not give your puppy an opportunity to learn that he can eliminate in the house. If an accident occurs you must correct the puppy when he is in the act of relieving himself. A puppy does not understand what you are talking about when you reprimand him for something he did even minutes before. Reprimand at the time of the act or not at all. Your housetraining chores will be reduced considerably if you avoid bad habits beginning in the first place.

If you are not able to watch your puppy every minute, he should be in his cage or crate with the door securely latched. Each time you put your puppy in the crate, give him a small treat of some kind. Throw the treat to the back of the cage and encourage the puppy to walk in on his own. When he does so, praise the puppy and perhaps hand him another piece of the treat through the wires of the cage.

If you can't watch your puppy while he is outside, keep him safely secured in his cage or crate to prevent him from getting into danger.

Do understand that a Saint puppy of 8 to 12 weeks of age will not be able to contain himself for long periods of time. Puppies of that age must relieve themselves often, except at night. Never leave a very young puppy in a crate for more than three hours during the day. Your schedule must be adjusted accordingly. Also make sure your puppy has relieved himself at night before the last member of the family retires.

Your first priority in the morning is to get the puppy outdoors. Just how early this will take place will depend much more on your puppy than on you. If your Saint puppy is like most others, there will be no doubt in your mind when he needs to be let out. You will also very quickly learn to tell the difference between the puppy's "emergency" signals and mere unhappy grumbling. Do not test the young puppy's ability to contain himself. His vocal demand to be let out is confirmation that the housebreaking lesson is being learned.

BASIC TRAINING

The Saint is a ready, willing, and eager student during training sessions. Saints, like all dogs, enjoy this special time with their master. Make sure you are in the right frame of mind for training sessions. Training should never take place when you are irritated, distressed, or preoccupied. Nor should you begin basic training in crowded or noisy places that will interfere with you or your dog's concentration. Once the commands are understood and learned you can begin testing your dog in public places, but at first the two of you should work in a place where you can concentrate fully on each other.

The "No!" Command

The most important command your Saint puppy will ever learn is the meaning of "no!" This is the command that the puppy can begin learning the minute he first arrives in your home. It is not necessary to frighten the puppy into learning the meaning of the "no" command, but it is critical that you never give this or any other command that you are not prepared and able to enforce. The only way a puppy learns to obey commands is to realize that once they are issued, commands must be complied with.

Leash Training

It is never too early to accustom your Saint puppy to his leash and collar. The leash and collar are your failsafe way of keeping your dog under control. It may not be necessary for the puppy or adult Saint to wear his collar and identification tags within the confines of your home, but no dog should ever leave home without a collar and without the leash held securely in your hand. In some countries it is the law.

It is best to begin getting your puppy accustomed to his collar by leaving a soft collar around his neck for a few minutes at a time. Gradually extend the time you leave the collar on your puppy. Most Saint puppies become accustomed to their collar very quickly and, after a few scratches in an attempt to remove it, forget they are even wearing one.

While you are playing with the puppy, attach a lightweight leash to the collar. Do not try to guide the puppy at first. The point here is to accustom the puppy to the feeling of having something attached to the collar.

Encourage your puppy to follow you as you move away. If the puppy is reluctant to cooperate, coax him along with a treat of some kind. Hold the treat in front of the puppy's nose to encourage him to follow you. Just as soon as the puppy takes a few steps toward you, praise him enthusiastically and continue to do so as you continue to move along.

The leash and collar are a means of keeping your Saint under control. Give him some time to get used to the unfamiliar feel.

Make the initial sessions short and fun. Continue the lessons in your home or yard until the puppy is completely unconcerned about the fact that he is on a leash. With a treat in one hand and the leash in the other, you can begin to use both to guide the puppy in the direction you wish to go. Begin your first walks in front of the house and eventually extend them down the street and around the block.

The Come Command

The next most important lesson for the Saint puppy to learn is to come when called. Therefore, it is very important that the puppy learn his name as soon as possible. Constantly repeating the dog's name is what does the trick. Use the puppy's name every time you speak to him: "Want to go outside, Rex?" "Come Rex, come!"

Learning to come on command could save your Saint's life when the two of you venture out into the world. "Come" is the command that a dog must obey without question, but the dog should not associate the command with fear. Your dog's response to his name and the word "come" should always be associated with a pleasant experience, such as great praise and petting or a food treat.

All too often, novice trainers get very angry at their dog for not responding immediately to the come command. When the dog finally does come, or after a chase, the owner scolds the dog for not obeying. The dog begins to associate "come" with an unpleasant result.

It is much easier to avoid establishing bad habits than it is to correct them once they are set. Avoid at all costs giving the come command unless you are sure your puppy will come to you. The very young puppy is far more inclined to learn the come command easily than the older dog. Use the command initially when the puppy is already on his way to you, or give the command while walking or running away from the youngster. Clap your hands and sound very happy and excited about having the puppy join in on this "game."

The very young Saint will normally want to stay as close to his owner as possible, especially in strange surroundings. When your puppy sees you moving away, his natural inclination will be to get close to you. This is a perfect time to use the come command.

Later, as a puppy grows more self-confident and independent, you may want to attach a long leash or rope to the puppy's collar to ensure the correct response. Again, do not chase or punish your puppy for not obeying the come command. Doing so in the initial stages of training makes the youngster associate the command with something to fear, and this will result in avoidance rather than the immediate positive response you desire. It is imperative that you praise your puppy and give him a treat when he does come to you, even if he voluntarily delays responding for many minutes.

The Sit and Stay Commands

The sit and stay commands are just as important to your Saint's safety (and your sanity) as the no command and learning to come when called. Many Saint puppies learn the sit command easily, often in just a few minutes, especially if it appears to be a game and a food treat is involved.

The come command is one of the most important commands that your puppy will learn. Be sure to associate it with positive things like treats and praise.

Your puppy should always be on collar and leash for his lessons. Young puppies are not beyond getting up and walking away when they have

decided that you and your lessons are boring. Do not test a very young puppy's patience to the limit. As good as the Saint Bernard is, remember that you are dealing with a baby. The attention span of any youngster, canine or human, is relatively short.

Give the sit command immediately before pushing down on your puppy's hindquarters or scooping his hind legs under the dog and molding him into a sit position. Praise the puppy lavishly when he does sit, even though it is you who made the action take place. Again, a food treat always seems to get the lesson across to the learning youngster.

Continue holding the dog's rear end down and repeat the sit command several times. If your dog makes an attempt to get up, repeat the command yet again while exerting pressure on the rear end until the correct position is assumed. Make your Saint stay in this position for increasing lengths of time. Begin with a few seconds and increase the time as lessons progress over the following weeks.

If your young student attempts to get up or lie down, he should be corrected by simply saying, "sit!" in a firm voice. This should be accompanied by returning the dog to the desired position. Only when you decide that your dog should get up should he be allowed to do so.

When you do decide your puppy can get up, call his name, say "OK," and make a big fuss over him. Praise and a food treat are in order every time your puppy responds correctly. Continue to help your puppy assume proper positions or respond to commands until he performs on his own. This way the puppy always wins—he gets it right every time. You are training with positive reinforcement.

Once your puppy has mastered the sit lesson, you may start on the stay command. With your dog on leash and facing you, command him to sit, then take a step or two back. If your dog attempts to get up to follow firmly say, "Sit, stay!" While you are saying this, raise your hand, palm toward the dog, and again command, "Stay!"

This Saint demonstrates the sit command with ease. Any attempt on your dog's part to get up must be corrected at once, returning him to the sit position and repeating, "Stay!" Once your Saint begins to understand what you want, you can gradually increase the distance you step back. With a long leash attached to your dog's collar (even a clothesline will do) start with a few steps and gradually increase the distance to several yards. Your Saint must eventually learn that the "Sit, stay" command must be obeyed no matter how far away you are. Later on, with advanced training, your dog will learn that the command is to be obeyed even when you move entirely out of sight.

As your Saint masters this lesson and is able to remain in the sit position for as long as you dictate, avoid calling your dog to you at first. This makes the dog overly anxious to get up and run to you. Instead, walk back to your dog and say "OK" which is a signal that the command is over. Later, when your Saint becomes more reliable in this respect, you can call him to you.

It is best to keep the "stay" part of the lesson to a minimum until the puppy is at least five or six months old. Everything in a very young Saint's makeup urges him to stay close to you wherever you go. The puppy has bonded to you, and forcing him to operate against his natural instincts can be bewildering.

The "Down" Command

Once your Saint has mastered the sit and stay commands, you may begin working on the down command. This is the single-word command that will tell your dog to lie down. Use the down command only when you want the dog to lie down. If you want your dog to get off your sofa or to stop jumping up on people, use the off command. Do not interchange these two commands. Doing so will only serve to confuse your dog, and evoking the right response will become next to impossible.

The down position is especially useful if you want your Saint to remain in a particular place for a long period of time. A dog is usually far more inclined to stay put when he is lying down than when he is sitting.

Teaching this command to your Saint may take a little more time and patience than the previous lessons. It is believed by some animal behaviorists that assuming the down position somehow represents submission to the dog. However, as far as most Saint owners are concerned, lying down is the position most Saints prefer, and keeping them in the sit position is often more difficult than the down.

With your Saint sitting in front of and facing you, hold a treat in your right hand and the excess part of the leash in your left hand. Hold the treat under the dog's nose and slowly bring your hand down to the ground. Your dog will follow the treat with his head and neck. As he does, give the command "Down" and exert light pressure on the dog's shoulders with your left hand. If your dog resists the pressure on his shoulders, do not continue pushing down. This will only create more resistance.

The down command can be difficult for some dogs to master, because it puts them in a submissive position. These Saints have no problem showing off what they've learned.

An alternative method of getting your Saint into the down position is to move around to the dog's right side and, as you draw his attention downward with your right hand, slide your left arm under the dog's front legs and gently slide them forward. Sometimes, this is easier to accomplish if you are kneeling.

As your Saint's forelegs begin to slide out to the front, keep moving the treat along the ground until the dog's whole body is lying on the ground, while you continually repeat "Down." Once your Saint has assumed the position you desire, give him the treat and a lot of praise. Continue assisting your dog into the "down" position until he does so on his own. Be firm and patient.

The "Heel" Command

In learning to heel, your Saint will walk on your left side with his shoulder next to your leg no matter which direction you might go or how quickly you turn. It is also very important for your dog to understand this command when the two of you are out walking. Teaching your Saint to heel will not only make your daily walks far more enjoyable, it will make him a far more tractable companion when the two of you are in crowded or confusing situations. Many uninformed people are frightened when they see a Saint coming down the street. A Saint lunging at the end of his leash, even he is just greeting the passersby, can be extremely intimidating.

We have found a lightweight, link-chain training collar to be very useful for the heeling lesson. It provides both quick pressure around the neck and a snapping sound, both of which get the dog's attention. Erroneously referred to as a "choke collar," the link-chain collar, when used properly, does not choke the dog. The pet shop at which you purchase the training collar will be able to show you the proper way to put the collar on your dog. Do not leave the collar on your puppy when training sessions are finished. Because the collars fit loosely, they can get hooked and cause injury or even death. As your puppy grows larger, you'll want a sturdier leash as well. We recommend a six-foot long leash, about three-fourths to one inch wide, made of leather or sturdy nylon.

When teaching your dog to heel, use a lightweight link-chain training collar. Be sure to remove the collar once the session is over.

Speaking in a clear, firm tone of voice will help your Saint understand his command much easier. Ch. Castor v. Hochkreuz, owned by the author, stands at attention.

As you train your puppy to walk along on the leash, you should accustom the youngster to walk on your left side. The leash should cross your body from the dog's collar to your right hand. The excess portion of the leash will be folded into your right hand, and your left hand on the leash will be used to make corrections with the leash.

A quick, short jerk on the leash with your left hand will keep your dog from lunging side to side, pulling ahead, or lagging back. As you make a correction, give the "heel" command. Keep the leash slack as long as your dog maintains the proper position at your side.

If your dog begins to drift away, give the leash a sharp jerk, guide the dog back to the correct position, and give the "heel" command. Do not pull on the leash with steady pressure. What is needed is a sharp but gentle jerking motion to get your dog's attention.

TRAINING CLASSES

As we mentioned before, the Saint is only limited in his education by you. There are few limits to what a patient, consistent owner can teach his or her Saint. For advanced obedience work beyond the basics, it is wise for the Saint owner to consider local professional assistance. Professional trainers have had longstanding experience in avoiding the pitfalls of obedience training and can help you to avoid these mistakes as well. Saint owners who have never trained a dog before have found that with professional assistance their dog can become quite a star.

Having your dog know the basic commands can make your time together more enjoyable and rewarding.

This training assistance can be obtained in many ways. Classes are particularly good for your Saint's socialization. The dog will learn that he must obey even when there are other dogs and people around. These classes also keep the Saint ever mindful of the fact that he must get along with other people and other dogs. There are inexpensive classes at many parks and recreation facilities, as well as very formal and sometimes very expensive individual lessons with private trainers.

There are also some obedience schools that will train your Saint for you. A Saint can and will learn with any good professional. However, unless your schedule provides no time at all to train your own dog, having someone else train the dog for you is not recommended. The rapport that develops between the owner who has trained his or her Saint to be a pleasant companion and good canine citizen and the dog is very special—well worth the time and patience it requires to achieve.

FUN AND GAMES

There are many opportunities for you to spend quality time with your Saint that will provide exercise for both of you and valuable training for your dog. In addition to conformation show ring competitions, the AKC and UKC offer obedience classes, agility events, and tracking tests. For the Saint, there is weight-pulling and an endless array of hiking and backpacking activities.

Owning a Saint is like having a best friend. This friend, however, loves doing anything and everything you enjoy, when and where you want to do it. Could you ask for more?

SPORT of Purebred Dogs

Welcome to the exciting and sometimes frustrating sport of dogs. No doubt you are trying to learn more about dogs or you wouldn't be deep into this book. This section covers the basics that may entice you, further your knowledge and help you to understand the dog world.

Dog showing has been a very popular sport for a long time and has been taken quite seriously by some. Others only enjoy it as a hobby.

The Kennel Club in England was formed in 1859, the American Kennel Club was established in 1884 and the Canadian Kennel Club was formed in 1888. The purpose of these clubs was to

Sugar Bear of Paradise at 20 months of age, owned and shown by Roy Stenmark.

register purebred dogs and maintain their Stud Books. In the beginning, the concept of registering dogs was not readily accepted. More than 36 million dogs have been enrolled in the AKC Stud Book since its inception in 1888. Presently the kennel clubs not only register dogs but adopt and enforce rules and regulations governing dog shows, obedience trials and field trials. Over the years they have fostered and encouraged interest in the health and welfare of the purebred dog. They routinely donate funds to veterinary research for study on genetic disorders.

Below are the addresses of the kennel clubs in the United States, Great Britain and Canada.

The American Kennel Club
260 Madison Avenue
New York, NY 10016
(Their registry is located at: 5580 Centerview Drive, STE 200, Raleigh, NC 27606-3390)

The Kennel Club
1 Clarges Street
Piccadilly, London, WIY 8AB, England

The Canadian Kennel Club
100-89 Skyway Avenue
Etobicoke, Ontario M6S 4V7
Canada

Today there are numerous activities that are enjoyable for
both the dog and the handler. Some of the activities include
conformation showing, obedience competition, tracking, agility,
the Canine Good Citizen Certificate, and a wide range of instinct
tests that vary from breed to breed. Where you start depends
upon your goals which early on may not be readily apparent.

Puppy Kindergarten

Every puppy will benefit from this class. PKT is the
foundation for all future dog activities from conformation to
"couch potatoes." Pet owners should make an effort to attend
even if they never expect
to show their dog. The
class is designed for
puppies about three
months of age with
graduation at approx-
imately five months of age.
All the puppies will be in
the same age group and,

*Ch. Cypress Woods Baccarat
winning Best of Breed at the 1980
S.B.C.A. National Specialty under
the author, handled by Hazel
(Lovey) Olbrich for owner/
breeder Betty Young. The late
Anna Gainsley, President of the
S.B.C.A., is presenting the trophy.*

Puppy kindergarten can help your Saint puppy learn the rules of basic obedience while at the same time socialize him with other dogs.

even though some may be a little unruly, there should not be any real problem. This class will teach the puppy some beginning obedience. As in all obedience classes the owner learns how to train his own dog. The PKT class gives the puppy the opportunity to interact with other puppies in the same age group and exposes him to strangers, which is very important. Some dogs grow up with behavior problems, one of them being fear of strangers. As you can see, there can be much to gain from this class.

There are some basic obedience exercises that every dog should learn. Some of these can be started with puppy kindergarten.

Recall

This quite possibly is the most important exercise you will ever teach. It should be a pleasant experience. The puppy may learn to do random recalls while being attached to a long line such as a clothes line. Later the exercise will start with the dog sitting and staying until called. The command is "Beau, come." Let your command be happy. You want your dog to come willingly and faithfully. The recall could save his life if he sneaks out the door. In practicing the recall, let him jump on you or touch you before you reach for him. If he is shy, then kneel down to his level. Reaching for the insecure dog could frighten him, and he may not be willing to come again in the future. Lots of praise and a treat would be in order whenever you do a recall. Under no circumstances should you ever correct your dog when he has come to you. Later in formal obedience your dog will be required to sit in front of you after recalling and then go to heel position.

CONFORMATION

Conformation showing is our oldest dog show sport. This type of showing is based on the dog's appearance—that is his structure, movement and attitude. When considering this type of showing, you need to be aware of your breed's standard and be able to evaluate your dog compared to that standard. The breeder of your puppy or other experienced breeders would be good sources for such an evaluation. Puppies can go through lots of changes over a period of time. Many puppies start out as promising hopefuls and then after maturing may be disappointing as show candidates. Even so this should not deter them from being excellent pets.

Usually conformation training classes are offered by the local kennel or obedience clubs. These are excellent places for training puppies. The puppy should be able to walk on a lead before entering such a class. Proper ring procedure and technique for posing (stacking) the dog will be demonstrated as well as gaiting the dog. Usually certain patterns are used in the ring such as the triangle or the "L." Conformation class, like the PKT class, will give your youngster the opportunity to socialize with different breeds of dogs and humans too.

It takes some time to learn the routine of conformation showing. Usually one starts at the puppy matches that may be AKC Sanctioned or Fun Matches. These matches are generally for puppies from two or three months to a year old, and there may be classes for the adult over the age of 12 months. Similar to point shows, the classes are divided by sex and after completion of the classes in that breed or variety, the class winners compete for Best of Breed or Variety. The winner goes on to compete in the Group and the Group winners compete for Best in Match. No championship points are awarded for match wins.

A few matches can be great training for puppies even though there is no intention to go on showing. Matches enable the puppy to meet new people and be handled by a stranger– the judge. It is also a change of environment, which broadens the horizon for both dog and handler. Matches and other dog activities boost the confidence of the handler and especially the younger handlers.

Mill Creek's Zebulon Pike was Best of Winners under the author at the 1980 S.B.C.A. National Specialty.

Earning an AKC championship is built on a point system, which is different from Great Britain. To become an AKC Champion of Record the dog must earn 15 points. The number of points earned each time depends upon the number of dogs in competition. The

number of points available at each show depends upon the breed, its sex and the location of the show. The United States is divided into ten AKC zones. Each zone has its own set of points. The purpose of the zones is to try to equalize the points available from breed to breed and area to area.The AKC adjusts the point scale annually.

The number of points that can be won at a show are between one and five. Three-, four- and five-point wins are considered majors. Not only does the dog need 15 points won under three different judges, but those points must include two majors under two different judges. Canada also works on a point system but majors are not required.

Dogs always show before bitches. The classes available to those seeking points are: Puppy (which may be divided into 6 to 9 months and 9 to 12 months); 12 to 18 months; Novice; Bred-by-Exhibitor; American-bred; and Open. The class winners of the same sex of each breed or variety compete against each other for Winners Dog and Winners Bitch. A Reserve Winners Dog and Reserve Winners Bitch are also awarded but do not carry any points unless the Winners win is disallowed by AKC. The Winners Dog and Bitch compete with the specials (those dogs that have attained championship) for Best of Breed or Variety, Best of Winners and Best of Opposite Sex. It is possible to pick up an extra point or even a major if the points are higher for the defeated winner than those of Best of Winners. The latter would get the higher total from the defeated winner.

At an all-breed show, each Best of Breed or Variety winner will go on to his respective Group and then the Group winners will compete against each other for Best in Show. There are seven Groups: Sporting, Hounds, Working, Terriers, Toys, Non-Sporting and Herding. Obviously there are no Groups at speciality shows (those shows that have only one breed or a show such as the American Spaniel Club's Flushing Spaniel Show, which is for all flushing spaniel breeds).

Earning a championship in England is somewhat different since they do not have a point system. Challenge Certificates are awarded if the judge feels the dog is deserving regardless of the number of dogs in competition. A dog must earn three Challenge Certificates under three different judges, with at least one of these Certificates being won after the age of 12 months. Competition is very strong and entries may be higher than they are in the US. The Kennel Club's Challenge Certificates are only available at Championship Shows.

In England, The Kennel Club regulations require that certain dogs, Border Collies and Gundog breeds, qualify in a working capacity (i.e., obedience or field trials) before becoming a full Champion. If they do not qualify in the working aspect, then they are designated a Show Champion, which is equivalent to the AKC's Champion of Record. A Gundog may be granted the title of Field Trial Champion (FT Ch.) if it passes all the tests in the field but would also have to qualify in conformation before becoming a full Champion. A Border Collie that earns the title of Obedience Champion (Ob Ch.) must also qualify in the conformation ring before becoming a Champion.

A puppy or dog is judged on his structure, movement, and attitude in a conformation show, which is the oldest dog show sport.

The US doesn't have a designation full Champion but does award for Dual and Triple Champions. The Dual Champion must be a Champion of Record, and either Champion Tracker, Herding Champion, Obedience Trial Champion or Field Champion. Any dog that has been awarded the titles of Champion of Record, and any two of the following: Champion Tracker, Herding Champion, Obedience Trial Champion or Field Champion, may be designated as a Triple Champion.

The shows in England seem to put more emphasis on breeder judges than those in the US. There is much competition within the breeds. Therefore the quality of the individual breeds should be very good. In the United States we tend to have more "all around judges" (those that judge multiple breeds) and use the breeder judges at the specialty shows. Breeder judges are more familiar with their own breed since they are actively breeding that breed or did so at one time. Americans emphasize Group and Best in Show wins and promote them accordingly.

The shows in England can be very large and extend over several days, with the Groups being scheduled on different days. Though multi-day shows are not common in the U.S., there are cluster shows, where several different clubs will use the same show site over consecutive days.

Westminster Kennel Club is our most prestigious show although the entry is limited to 2500. In recent years, entry has been limited to Champions. This show is more formal than the majority of the shows with the judges wearing formal attire and the handlers fashionably dressed. In most instances the

The Saint Bernard is a large dog that is not easy to control. Make sure your Saint masters basic obedience before taking him into the show ring.

quality of the dogs is superb. After all, it is a show of Champions. It is a good show to study the AKC registered breeds and is by far the most exciting—especially since it is televised! WKC is one of the few shows in this country that is still benched. This means the dog must be in his benched area during the show hours except when he is being groomed, in the ring, or being exercised.

Typically, the handlers are very particular about their appearances. They are careful not to wear something that will detract from their dog but will perhaps enhance it. American ring procedure is quite formal compared to that of other countries. There is a certain etiquette expected between the judge and exhibitor and among the other exhibitors. Of course it is not always the case but the judge is supposed to be polite, not engaging in small talk or acknowledging how well he knows the handler. There is a more informal and relaxed atmosphere at the shows in other countries. For instance, the dress code is more casual. I can see where this might be more fun for the exhibitor and especially for the novice. The U.S. is very handler-oriented in many of the breeds. It is true, in most instances, that the experienced professional handler can present the dog better and will have a feel for what a judge likes.

In England, Crufts is The Kennel Club's own show and is most assuredly the largest dog show in the world. They've been known to have an entry of nearly 20,000, and the show lasts four days. Entry is only gained by qualifying through winning in specified classes at another Championship Show.

Westminster is strictly conformation, but Crufts exhibitors and spectators enjoy not only conformation but obedience, agility and a multitude of exhibitions as well. Obedience was admitted in 1957 and agility in 1983.

If you are handling your own dog, please give some consideration to your apparel. For sure the dress code at matches is more informal than the point shows. However, you should wear something a little more appropriate than beach attire or ragged jeans and bare feet. If you check out the handlers and see what is presently fashionable, you'll catch on. Men usually dress with a shirt and tie and a nice sports coat. Whether you are male or female, you will want to wear comfortable clothes and shoes. You need to be able to run with your dog and you certainly don't want to take a chance of falling and hurting yourself. Heaven forbid, if nothing else, you'll upset your dog. Women usually wear a dress or two-piece outfit, preferably with pockets to carry bait, comb, brush, etc. In this case men are the lucky ones with all their pockets. Ladies, think about where your dress

Two-year-old Lux-Linksmader, owned by Betty-Anne Stenmark.

Showing your dog requires a lot of preparation. Bring along all the necessary equipment needed for a show, including a table and grooming tools.

will be if you need to kneel on the floor and also think about running. Does it allow freedom to do so?

You need to take along dog; crate; ex pen (if you use one); extra newspaper; water pail and water; all required grooming equipment, including hair dryer and extension cord; table; chair for you; bait for dog and lunch for you and friends; and, last but not least, clean up materials, such as plastic bags, paper towels, and perhaps a bath towel and some shampoo—just in case. Don't forget your entry confirmation and directions to the show.

If you are showing in obedience, then you will want to wear pants. Many of our top obedience handlers wear pants that are color-coordinated with their dogs. The philosophy is that imperfections in the black dog will be less obvious next to your black pants.

Whether you are showing in conformation, Junior Showmanship or obedience, you need to watch the clock and be sure you are not late. It is customary to pick up your conformation armband a few minutes before the start of the class. They will not wait for you and if you are on the show grounds and not in the ring, you will upset everyone. It's a little more complicated picking up your obedience armband if you show later in the class. If you have not picked up your armband and they get to your number, you may not be allowed to show. It's best to pick up your armband early, but then you may show earlier than expected if other handlers don't pick up. Customarily all conflicts should be discussed with the judge prior to the start of the class.

Junior Showmanship

The Junior Showmanship Class is a wonderful way to build self confidence even if there are no aspirations of staying with the dog-show game later in life. Frequently, Junior Showmanship becomes the background of those who become successful exhibitors/handlers in the future. In some instances it is taken very seriously, and success is measured in terms of wins. The Junior Handler is judged solely on his ability and skill in presenting his dog. The dog's conformation is not to be considered by the judge. Even so the condition and grooming of the dog may be a reflection upon the handler.

Usually the matches and point shows include different classes. The Junior Handler's dog may be entered in a breed or obedience class and even shown by another person in that class. Junior Showmanship classes are usually divided by age and perhaps sex. The age is determined by the handler's age on the day of the show. The classes are:

Novice Junior for those at least ten and under 14 years of age who at time of entry closing have not won three first places in a Novice Class at a licensed or member show.

Novice Senior for those at least 14 and under 18 years of age who at the time of entry closing have not won three first places in a Novice Class at a licensed or member show.

Open Junior for those at least ten and under 14 years of age who at the time of entry closing have won at least three first places in a Novice Junior Showmanship Class at a licensed or member show with competition present.

Open Senior for those at least 14 and under 18 years of age who at time of entry closing have won at least three first places in a Novice Junior Showmanship Class at a licensed or member show with competition present.

Junior Handlers must include their AKC Junior Handler number on each show entry. This needs to be obtained from the AKC.

CANINE GOOD CITIZEN

The AKC sponsors a program to encourage dog owners to train their dogs. Local clubs perform the pass/fail tests, and dogs who pass are awarded a Canine Good Citizen Certificate. Proof of vaccination is required at the time of participation. The test includes:

1. Accepting a friendly stranger.
2. Sitting politely for petting.
3. Appearance and grooming.
4. Walking on a loose leash.
5. Walking through a crowd.
6. Sit and down on command/staying in place.
7. Come when called.
8. Reaction to another dog.
9. Reactions to distractions.
10. Supervised separation.

If more effort was made by pet owners to accomplish these exercises, fewer dogs would be cast off to the humane shelter.

OBEDIENCE

Obedience is necessary, without a doubt, but it can also become a

Junior showmanship is a great way to build self-confidence and have fun, too. These kids have a blast at a children's handling class held at a Saint Bernard Club Fun Day.

wonderful hobby or even an obsession. Obedience classes and competition can provide wonderful companionship, not only with your dog but with your classmates or fellow competitors. It is always gratifying to discuss your dog's problems with others who have had similar experiences. The AKC acknowledged Obedience around 1936, and it has changed tremendously even though many of the exercises are basically the same. Today, obedience competition is just that—very competitive. Even so, it is possible for every obedience exhibitor to come home a winner (by earning qualifying scores) even though he/she may not earn a placement in the class.

A dog needs to meet certain requirements, such as sitting politely and accepting friendly strangers, in order to receive a Canine Good Citizen Certificate.

Most of the obedience titles are awarded after earning three qualifying scores (legs) in the appropriate class under three different judges. These classes offer a perfect score of 200, which is extremely rare. Each of the class exercises has its own point value. A leg is earned after receiving a score of at least 170 and at least 50 percent of the points available in each exercise. The titles are:

Companion Dog—CD

This is called the Novice Class and the exercises are:

1. Heel on leash and figure 8	40 points
2. Stand for examination	30 points
3. Heel free	40 points
4. Recall	30 points
5. Long sit—one minute	30 points
6. Long down—three minutes	30 points
Maximum total score	200 points

Companion Dog Excellent—CDX

This is the Open Class and the exercises are:

1. Heel off leash and figure 8	40 points
2. Drop on recall	30 points
3. Retrieve on flat	20 points
4. Retrieve over high jump	30 points
5. Broad jump	20 points
6. Long sit—three minutes (out of sight)	30 points
7. Long down—five minutes (out of sight)	30 points
Maximum total score	200 points

Utility Dog—UD

The Utility Class exercises are:

1. Signal Exercise	40 points
2. Scent discrimination-Article 1	30 points
3. Scent discrimination-Article 2	30 points
4. Directed retrieve	30 points
5. Moving stand and examination	30 points
6. Directed jumping	40 points
Maximum total score	200 points

After achieving the UD title, you may feel inclined to go after the UDX and/or OTCh. The UDX (Utility Dog Excellent) title went into effect in January 1994. It is not easily attained. The title requires qualifying simultaneously ten times in Open B and Utility B but not necessarily at consecutive shows.

The OTCh (Obedience Trial Champion) is awarded after the dog has earned his UD and then goes on to earn 100 championship points, a first place in Utility, a first place in Open and another first place in either class. The placements must be won under three different judges at all-breed obedience trials. The points are determined by the number of dogs competing in the Open B and Utility B classes. The OTCh title precedes the dog's name.

Obedience matches (AKC Sanctioned, Fun, and Show and Go) are usually available. Usually they are sponsored by the local obedience clubs. When preparing an obedience dog for a title, you will find matches very helpful. Fun Matches and Show and Go Matches are more lenient in allowing you to make corrections in the ring. This type of training is usually very necessary for the Open and Utility Classes. AKC Sanctioned

A well-trained and even-tempered Saint can participate in any activity. Two-year-old Katelynn enjoys riding her "horse."

Obedience Matches do not allow corrections in the ring since they must abide by the AKC Obedience Regulations. If you are interested in showing in obedience, then you should contact the AKC for a copy of the Obedience Regulations.

TRACKING

Tracking is officially classified obedience. There are three tracking titles available: Tracking Dog (TD), Tracking Dog Excellent (TDX), Variable Surface Tracking (VST). If all three tracking titles are obtained, then the dog officially becomes a CT (Champion Tracker). The CT will go in front of the dog's name.

A TD may be earned anytime and does not have to follow the other obedience titles. There are many exhibitors that prefer tracking to obedience, and there are others who do both.

Tracking Dog–TD

A dog must be certified by an AKC tracking judge that he is ready to perform in an AKC test. The AKC can provide the names of tracking judges in your area that you can contact for certification. Depending on where you live, you may have to travel a distance if there is no local tracking judge. The certification track will be equivalent to a regular AKC track. A regulation track must be 440 to 500 yards long with at least two right-angle turns out in the open. The track will be aged 30 minutes to two hours. The handler has two starting flags at the beginning of the track to indicate the direction started. The dog works on a harness and 40-foot lead

Showing will be much more rewarding for both dog and owner if your Saint enjoys and feels comfortable competing in the ring.

and must work at least 20 feet in front of the handler. An article (either a dark glove or wallet) will be dropped at the end of the track, and the dog must indicate it but not necessarily retrieve it.

People always ask what the dog tracks. Initially, the beginner on the short-aged track tracks the tracklayer. Eventually the dog learns to track the disturbed vegetation and learns to differentiate between tracks. Getting started with tracking requires reading the AKC regulations and a good book on tracking plus finding other tracking enthusiasts. Work on the buddy system. That is—lay tracks for each other so you can practice blind tracks. It is possible to train on your own, but if

you are a beginner, it is a lot more entertaining to track with a buddy. It's rewarding seeing the dog use his natural ability.

Tracking Dog Excellent–TDX

The TDX track is 800 to 1000 yards long and is aged three to five hours. There will be five to seven turns. An article is left at the starting flag, and three other articles must be indicated on the track. There is only one flag at the start, so it is a blind start. Approximately one and a half hours after the track is laid, two tracklayers will cross over the track at two different places to test the dog's ability to stay with the original track. There will be at least two obstacles on the track such as a change of cover, fences, creeks, ditches, etc. The dog must have a TD before entering a TDX. There is no certification required for a TDX.

Variable Surface Tracking–VST

This test came into effect September 1995. The dog must have a TD earned at least six months prior to entering this test. The track is 600 to 800 yards long and shall have a minimum of three different surfaces. Vegetation shall be included along with two areas devoid of vegetation such as concrete, asphalt, gravel, sand, hard pan or mulch. The areas devoid of vegetation shall comprise at least one-third to one-half of the track. The track is aged three to five hours. There will be four to eight turns and four numbered articles including one leather, one plastic, one metal and one fabric dropped on the track. There is one starting flag. The handler will work at least 10 feet from the dog.

AGILITY

Agility was first introduced by John Varley in England at the Crufts Dog Show, February 1978, but Peter Meanwell,

Performance events give your Saint the opportunity to use his natural abilities.

competitor and judge, actually developed the idea. It was officially recognized in the early '80s. Agility is extremely popular in England and Canada and growing in popularity in the U.S. The AKC acknowledged agility in August

Training your Saint for competition takes dedication and hard work. It also enables pet and owner to form a strong bond.

1994. Dogs must be at least 12 months of age to be entered. It is a fascinating sport that the dog, handler and spectators enjoy to the utmost. Agility is a spectator sport! The dog performs off lead. The handler either runs with his dog or positions himself on the course and directs his dog with verbal and hand signals over a timed course over or through a variety of obstacles including a time out or pause. One of the main drawbacks to agility is finding a place to train. The obstacles take up a lot of space and it is very time consuming to put up and take down courses.

The titles earned at AKC agility trials are Novice Agility Dog (NAD), Open Agility Dog (OAD), Agility Dog Excellent (ADX), and Master Agility Excellent (MAX). In order to acquire an agility title, a dog must earn a qualifying score in its respective class on three separate occasions under two different judges. The MAX will be awarded after earning ten qualifying scores in the Agility Excellent Class.

PERFORMANCE TESTS

During the last decade the American Kennel Club has promoted performance tests–those events that test the different breeds' natural abilities. This type of event encourages a handler to devote even more time to his dog and retain the natural instincts of his breed heritage. It is an important part of the wonderful world of dogs.

Whether or not you enter your Saint in competitions, the time that you spend training will provide him with both exercise and mental stimulation.

HEALTH CARE

Veterinary medicine has become far more sophisticated than what was available to our ancestors. This can be attributed to the increase in household pets and consequently the demand for better care for them. Also human medicine has become far more complex. Today diagnostic testing in veterinary medicine parallels human diagnostics. Because of better technology we can expect our pets to live healthier lives thereby increasing their life spans.

THE FIRST CHECKUP

You will want to take your new puppy/dog in for its first check up within 48 to 72 hours after acquiring it. Many breeders strongly recommend this checkup and so do the humane shelters. A puppy/dog can appear healthy but it may have a serious problem that is not

For a clean bill of health, take your puppy to the vet within 48 to 72 hours after acquiring him.

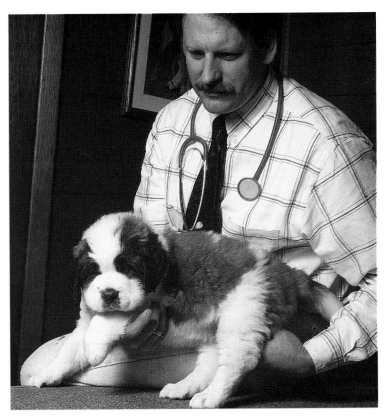

Do as much as you can to ensure the well-being of your Saint, such as choosing a good vet.

apparent to the layman. Most pets have some type of a minor flaw that may never cause a real problem.

Unfortunately if he/she should have a serious problem, you will want to consider the consequences of keeping the pet and the attachments that will be formed, which may be broken prematurely. Keep in mind there are many healthy dogs looking for good homes.

This first checkup is a good time to establish yourself with the veterinarian and learn the office policy regarding their hours and how they handle emergencies. Usually the breeder or another conscientious pet owner is a good reference for locating a capable veterinarian. You should be aware that not all veterinarians give the same quality of service. Please do not make your selection on the least expensive clinic, as they may be short changing your pet. There is the possibility that eventually it will cost you more due to improper diagnosis, treatment, etc. If you are selecting a new veterinarian, feel free to ask for a tour of the clinic. You should inquire about making an appointment for a tour since all clinics are working clinics, and therefore may not be available all day for sightseers. You may worry less if you see where your pet will be spending the day if he ever needs to be hospitalized.

The Physical Exam

Your veterinarian will check your pet's overall condition, which includes listening to the heart; checking the respiration; feeling the abdomen, muscles and joints; checking the mouth, which includes the gum color and signs of gum disease along with plaque buildup; checking the ears for signs of an infection or ear mites; examining the eyes; and, last but not least, checking the condition of the skin and coat.

He should ask you questions regarding your pet's eating and elimination habits and invite you to relay your questions. It is a good idea to prepare a list so as not to forget anything. He should discuss the proper diet and the quantity to be fed. If this should differ from your breeder's recommendation, then you should convey to him the breeder's choice and see if he approves. If he recommends changing the diet, then this should be done over a few days so as not to cause a gastrointestinal upset. It is customary to take in a fresh stool sample (just a small amount) for a test for intestinal parasites. It must be fresh, preferably within 12 hours, since the eggs hatch quickly and after hatching will not be observed under the microscope. If your pet isn't obliging then, usually the technician can take one in the clinic.

Immunizations

It is important that you take your puppy/dog's vaccination record with you on your first visit. In case of a puppy, presumably the breeder has seen to the vaccinations up to the time you acquired custody. Veterinarians differ in their vaccination protocol. It is not unusual for your puppy to have received vaccinations for distemper, hepatitis, leptospirosis, parvovirus and parainfluenza every two to three weeks from the age of five or six weeks. Usually this is a combined injection and is typically called the DHLPP. The DHLPP is given through at least 12 to 14 weeks of age, and it is customary to continue with another parvovirus vaccine at 16 to 18 weeks. You may wonder why so many immunizations are necessary. No one knows for sure when the puppy's maternal antibodies are gone, although it is customarily accepted that distemper antibodies are gone by 12 weeks. Usually parvovirus antibodies are gone by 16 to 18 weeks of age. However, it is possible for the maternal antibodies to be gone at a much earlier age or even a later age. Therefore immunizations are started at an early age. The vaccine will not give immunity as long as there are maternal antibodies.

On the initial visit, your vet should discuss with you the proper diet for your Saint puppy. If he suggests changing the pup's original diet, do so gradually.

The rabies vaccination is given at three or six months of age depending on your local laws. A vaccine for bordetella (kennel cough) is advisable and can be given anytime from the age of five weeks. The coronavirus is not commonly given unless there is a problem locally. The Lyme vaccine is necessary in endemic areas. Lyme disease has been reported in 47 states.

Distemper

This is virtually an incurable disease. If the dog recovers, he is subject to severe nervous disorders. The virus attacks every tissue in the body and resembles a bad cold with a fever. It can cause a runny nose and eyes and cause gastrointestinal disorders, including a poor appetite, vomiting and diarrhea. The virus is carried by raccoons, foxes, wolves, mink and other dogs. Unvaccinated youngsters and senior citizens are very susceptible. This is still a common disease.

Hepatitis

This is a virus that is most serious in very young dogs. It is spread by contact with an infected animal or its stool or urine. The virus affects the liver and kidneys and is characterized by high fever, depression and lack of appetite. Recovered animals may be afflicted with chronic illnesses.

Bordetella attached to canine cilia. Otherwise known as kennel cough, this disease is highly contagious and should be vaccinated against routinely.

Leptospirosis

This is a bacterial disease transmitted by contact with the urine of an infected dog, rat or other wildlife. It produces severe symptoms of fever, depression, jaundice and internal bleeding and was fatal before the vaccine was developed. Recovered dogs can be carriers, and the disease can be transmitted from dogs to humans.

Parvovirus

This was first noted in the late 1970s and is still a fatal disease. However, with proper vaccinations, early diagnosis and prompt treatment, it is a manageable disease. It attacks the bone marrow and intestinal tract. The symptoms include depression, loss of appetite, vomiting, diarrhea and collapse. Immediate medical attention is of the essence.

Rabies

This is shed in the saliva and is carried by raccoons, skunks, foxes, other dogs, and cats. It attacks nerve tissue, resulting in paralysis and death. Rabies can be transmitted to people and is virtually always fatal. This disease is reappearing in the suburbs.

Be careful not to let your Saint wander off when he is outside, so as to prevent contact with a rabid animal.

Bordetella (Kennel Cough)

The symptoms are coughing, sneezing, hacking and retching accompanied by nasal discharge usually lasting from a few days to several weeks. There are several disease-producing organisms responsible for this disease. The present vaccines are helpful but do not protect for all the strains. It usually is not life threatening but in some instances it can progress to a serious bronchopneumonia. The disease is highly contagious. The vaccination should be given routinely for dogs that come in contact with other dogs, such as through boarding, training class or visits to the groomer.

Coronavirus

This is usually self limiting and not life threatening. It was first noted in the late '70s about a year before parvovirus. The virus produces a yellow/brown stool and there may be depression, vomiting and diarrhea.

Lyme Disease

This was first diagnosed in the United States in 1976 in Lyme, CT in people who lived in close proximity to the deer tick. Symptoms may include acute lameness, fever, swelling of joints and loss of appetite. Your veterinarian can advise you if you live in an endemic area.

After your puppy has completed his puppy vaccinations, you will continue to booster the DHLPP once a year. It is customary to booster the rabies one year after the first vaccine and then, depending on where you live, it should be boostered every year or every three years. This depends on your local laws. The Lyme and corona vaccines are boostered annually and it is recommended that the bordetella be boostered every six to eight months.

ANNUAL VISIT

I would like to impress the importance of the annual check up, which would include the booster vaccinations, check for intestinal parasites and test for heartworm. Today in our very busy world it is rush, rush and see "how much you can get for how little." Unbelievably, some non-veterinary businesses have entered into the vaccination business. More harm than good can come to your dog through improper vaccinations, possibly from inferior vaccines and/or the wrong schedule. More than likely you truly care about your companion dog and over the years you have devoted much time and expense to his well being. Perhaps you are unaware that a vaccination is not just a vaccination. There is more involved. Please, please follow through with regular physical examinations. It is so important for your veterinarian to know your dog and this is especially true during middle age through the geriatric years. More than likely your older dog will require more

As your dog ages, his health needs will change. Keep veterinary visits regular and all vaccinations up-to-date.

All dogs have off days when they do not seem them-selves. However, if this lethargic condition persists, you should have your Saint examined by a Professional. than one physical a year. The annual physical is good preventive medicine. Through early diagnosis and subsequent treatment your dog can maintain a longer and better quality of life.

INTESTINAL PARASITES

Hookworms

These are almost microscopic intestinal worms that can cause anemia and therefore serious problems, including death, in young puppies. Hookworms can be transmitted to humans through penetration of the skin. Puppies may be born with them.

Roundworms

These are spaghetti-like worms that can cause a potbellied appearance and dull coat along with more severe symptoms, such as vomiting, diarrhea and coughing. Puppies acquire these while in the mother's uterus and through lactation. Both hookworms and roundworms may be acquired through ingestion.

Whipworms

These have a three-month life cycle and are not acquired through the dam. They cause intermittent diarrhea usually with mucus. Whipworms are possibly the most difficult worm to eradicate. Their eggs are very resistant to most environmental factors and can last for years until the proper conditions enable them to mature. Whipworms are seldom seen in the stool.

Roundworm eggs as seen on a fecal evaluation. The eggs must develop for at least 12 days before becoming infective.

Intestinal parasites are more prevalent in some areas than others. Climate, soil and contamination are big factors contributing to the incidence of intestinal parasites. Eggs are passed in the stool, lay on the ground and then become infective in a certain number of days. Each of the above worms has a different life cycle. Your best chance of becoming and remaining worm-free is to always pooper-scoop your yard. A fenced-in yard keeps stray dogs out, which is certainly helpful.

I would recommend having a fecal examination on your dog twice a year or more often if there is a problem. If your dog has a positive fecal sample, then he will be given the appropriate medication and you will be asked to bring back another stool sample in a certain period of time (depending on the type of worm) and then be rewormed. This process goes on until he has at least two negative samples. The different types of worms require different medications. You will be wasting your money and doing your dog an injustice by buying over-the-counter medication without first consulting your veterinarian.

OTHER INTERNAL PARASITES

Coccidiosis and Giardiasis

These protozoal infections usually affect puppies, especially in places where large numbers of puppies are brought together. Older dogs may harbor these infections but do not show signs unless they are stressed. Symptoms include diarrhea, weight loss and lack of appetite. These infections are not always apparent in the fecal examination.

Tapeworms

Seldom apparent on fecal floatation, they are diagnosed frequently as rice-like segments around the dog's anus and the base of the tail. Tapeworms are long, flat and ribbon like, sometimes several feet in length, and made up of many segments about five-eighths of an inch long. The two most common types of tapeworms found in the dog are:

(1) First the larval form of the flea tapeworm parasite must mature in an intermediate host, the flea, before it can become infective. Your dog acquires this by ingesting the flea through licking and chewing.

(2) Rabbits, rodents and certain large game animals serve as intermediate hosts for other species of tapeworms. If your dog should eat one of these infected hosts, then he can acquire tapeworms.

HEARTWORM DISEASE

This is a worm that resides in the heart and adjacent blood vessels of the lung that produces microfilaria, which circulate in the bloodstream. It is possible for a dog to be infected with any number of worms from one to a hundred that can be 6 to 14 inches long. It is a life-threatening disease, expensive to treat and easily prevented. Depending on where you live, your veterinarian may recommend a preventive year-round and either an annual or semiannual blood test. The most common preventive is given once a month.

EXTERNAL PARASITES

Fleas

These pests are not only the dog's worst enemy but also enemy to the owner's pocketbook. Preventing is less expensive than treating, but regardless we'd prefer to spend our money elsewhere. Likely, the majority of our dogs are allergic to the bite of a flea, and in many cases it only takes one flea bite. The protein in the flea's saliva is the culprit. Allergic dogs have a reaction, which usually results in a "hot spot." More than likely such a reaction will involve a trip to the veterinarian for treatment. Yes, prevention is less expensive. Fortunately today there are several good products available.

If there is a flea infestation, no one product is going to correct the problem. Not only will the dog require treatment so will the environment. In general flea collars are not very effective although there is now available an "egg" collar that will kill the eggs on the dog. Dips are the most economical but they are messy. There are some effective shampoos and treatments available through pet shops and veterinarians. An oral tablet arrived on the American market in 1995 and was popular in Europe the previous year. It sterilizes

If your Saint starts scratching after he has been outdoors, check his coat for infestation.

the female flea but will not kill adult fleas. Therefore the tablet, which is given monthly, will decrease the flea population but is not a "cure-all." Those dogs that suffer from flea-bite allergy will still be subjected to the bite of the flea. Another popular parasiticide is permethrin, which is applied to the back of the dog in one or two places depending on the dog's weight. This product works as a repellent causing the flea to get "hot feet" and jump off. Do not confuse this product with some of the organophosphates that are also applied to the dog's back.

Some products are not usable on young puppies. Treating fleas should be done under your veterinarian's guidance. Frequently it is necessary to combine products and the layman does not have the knowledge regarding possible toxicities. It is hard to believe but there are a few dogs that do have a natural resistance to fleas. Nevertheless it would be wise to treat all pets at the same time. Don't forget your cats. Cats just love to prowl the neighborhood and consequently return with unwanted guests.

Adult fleas live on the dog but their eggs drop off the dog into the environment. There they go through four larval stages before reaching adulthood,

All the pets in the household should be treated for fleas and ticks.

Regular medical care is essential throughout your Saint's adulthood. Annual checkups are a part of his lifelong maintenance. and thereby are able to jump back on the poor unsuspecting dog. The cycle resumes and takes between 21 to 28 days under ideal conditions. There are environmental products available that will kill both the adult fleas and the larvae.

Ticks

Ticks carry Rocky Mountain Spotted Fever, Lyme disease and can cause tick paralysis. They should be removed with tweezers, trying to pull out the head. The jaws carry disease. There is a tick preventive collar that does an excellent job. The ticks automatically back out on those dogs wearing collars.

Sarcoptic Mange

This is a mite that is difficult to find on skin scrapings. The pinnal reflex is a good indicator of this disease. Rub the ends of the pinna (ear) together and the dog will start scratching with his foot. Sarcoptes are highly contagious to other dogs and to humans although they do not live long on humans. They cause intense itching.

Demodectic Mange

A responsible breeder is concerned with the health and well-being of his or her dogs and may ask that you not breed your pet-quality Saint.

This is a mite that is passed from the dam to her puppies. It affects youngsters age three to ten months. Diagnosis is confirmed by skin scraping. Small areas of alopecia around the eyes, lips and/or forelegs become visible. There is little itching unless there is a secondary bacterial infection. Some breeds are afflicted more than others.

Cheyletiella

This causes intense itching and is diagnosed by skin scraping. It lives in the outer layers of the skin of dogs, cats, rabbits and humans. Yellow-gray scales may be found on the back and the rump, top of the head and the nose.

TO BREED OR NOT TO BREED

More than likely your breeder has requested that you have your puppy neutered or spayed. Your breeder's request is based on what is healthiest for your dog and what is most beneficial for your breed. Experienced and conscientious breeders devote many years into developing a bloodline. In order to do this, he makes every effort to plan each breeding in regard to conformation, temperament and health. This type of breeder does his best to perform the necessary testing (i.e., OFA, CERF, testing for inherited blood disorders, thyroid, etc.). Testing is expensive and sometimes very disheartening when a favorite dog doesn't pass his health tests. The health history pertains not only to the breeding stock but to the immediate ancestors. Reputable breeders do not want their offspring to be bred indiscriminately. Therefore you may be asked to neuter or spay your puppy. Of course there is always the exception, and your breeder may agree to let you breed your

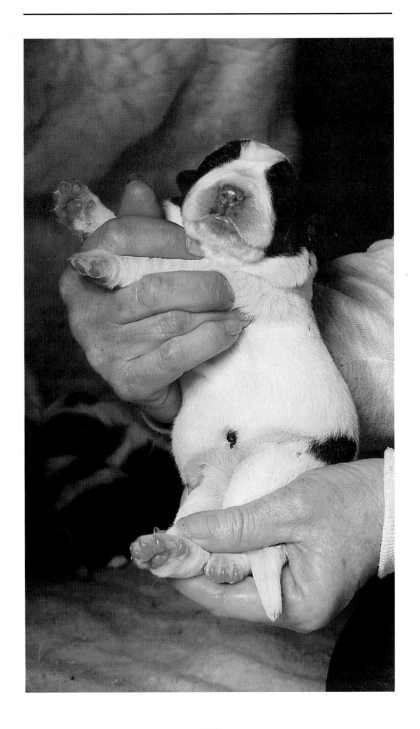

Spaying or neutering your dog reduces the risk of health problems later on in life.

dog under his direct supervision. This is an important concept. More and more effort is being made to breed healthier dogs.

Spay/Neuter

There are numerous benefits of performing this surgery at six months of age. Unspayed females are subject to mammary and ovarian cancer. In order to prevent mammary cancer she must be spayed prior to her first heat cycle. Later in life, an unspayed female may develop a pyometra (an infected uterus), which is definitely life threatening.

Spaying is performed under a general anesthetic and is easy on the young dog. As you might expect it is a little harder on the older dog, but that is no reason to deny her the surgery. The surgery removes the ovaries and uterus. It is important to remove all the ovarian tissue. If some is left behind, she could remain attractive to males. In order to view the ovaries, a reasonably long incision is necessary. An ovariohysterectomy is considered major surgery.

Neutering the male at a young age will inhibit some characteristic male behavior that owners frown upon. Some boys will not hike their legs and mark territory if they are neutered at six months of age. Also neutering at a young age has hormonal benefits, lessening the chance of hormonal aggressiveness.

Surgery involves removing the testicles but leaving the scrotum. If there should be a retained testicle, then he definitely needs to be neutered before the age of two or three years. Retained testicles can develop into cancer. Unneutered males are at risk for testicular cancer, perineal fistulas, perianal tumors and fistulas and prostatic disease.

Although some dogs may become a little less active immediately after spaying or neutering, it is usually temporary and not a cause for concern.

Intact males and females are prone to housebreaking accidents. Females urinate frequently before, during and after heat cycles, and males tend to mark territory if there is a female in heat. Males may show the same behavior if there is a visiting dog or guests.

Surgery involves a sterile operating procedure equivalent to human surgery. The incision site is shaved, surgically scrubbed and draped. The veterinarian wears a sterile surgical gown, cap, mask and gloves. Anesthesia should be monitored by a registered technician. It is customary for the veterinarian to recommend a pre-anesthetic blood screening, looking for metabolic problems and a ECG rhythm strip to check for normal heart function. Today anesthetics are equal to human anesthetics, which enables your dog to walk out of the clinic the same day as surgery.

Some folks worry about their dog gaining weight after being neutered or spayed. This is usually not the case. It is true that some dogs may be less active so they could develop a problem, but most dogs are just as active as they were before surgery. However, if your dog should begin to gain, then you need to decrease his food and see to it that he gets a little more exercise.

DENTAL CARE for Your Dog's Life

So you've got a new puppy! You also have a new set of puppy teeth in your household. Anyone who has ever raised a puppy is abundantly aware of these new teeth. Your puppy will chew anything it can reach, chase your shoelaces, and play "tear the rag" with any piece of clothing it can find. When puppies are newly born, they have no teeth. At about four weeks of age, puppies of most breeds begin to develop their deciduous or baby teeth. They begin eating semi-solid food, fighting and biting with their litter mates, and learning discipline from their mother. As their new teeth come in, they inflict more pain on their mother's breasts, so her feeding sessions become less frequent and shorter. By six or eight weeks, the mother will start growling to warn her pups when they are fighting too roughly or hurting her as they nurse too much with their new teeth.

Puppies need to chew. It is a necessary part of their physical and mental development. They develop muscles and necessary life skills as they drag objects around, fight over possession, and vocalize alerts and warnings. Puppies chew on things to explore their world. They are using their sense of taste to determine what is food and what is not. How else can they tell an electrical cord from a lizard? At about four months of age, most puppies begin shedding their baby teeth. Often these teeth need some help to come out and make way for the permanent teeth. The incisors (front teeth) will be replaced first. Then, the adult canine or fang teeth erupt. When the baby tooth is not shed before the permanent tooth comes in, veterinarians call it a retained deciduous tooth. This condition will often cause gum infections by trapping hair and debris between the permanent tooth and the retained baby tooth. Nylafloss® is an excellent device for puppies to use. They can toss it, drag it, and chew on the many surfaces it presents. The baby teeth can catch in the nylon material, aiding in their removal. Puppies that have adequate chew toys will have less destructive behavior, develop more physically, and have less chance of retained deciduous teeth.

During the first year, your dog should be seen by your veterinarian at regular intervals. Your veterinarian will let you know when to bring in your puppy for vaccinations and parasite examinations. At each visit, your veterinarian should inspect the lips, teeth, and mouth as part of a complete physical examination. You should take some part in the maintenance of your dog's oral health. You should examine your dog's mouth weekly throughout his first year to make sure there are no sores, foreign objects, tooth problems, etc. If your dog drools excessively, shakes its head, or has bad breath, consult your veterinarian. By the time your dog is six months old, the permanent teeth are all in and plaque can start to accumulate on the tooth surfaces. This is when your dog needs to develop good dental-care habits to prevent calculus build-up on its teeth. Brushing is best. That is a fact that cannot be denied. However, some dogs do not like their teeth brushed regularly, or you may not be able to accomplish the task. In that case, you should consider a product that will help prevent plaque and calculus build-up.

A complete oral exam should include the lips, teeth, and mouth.

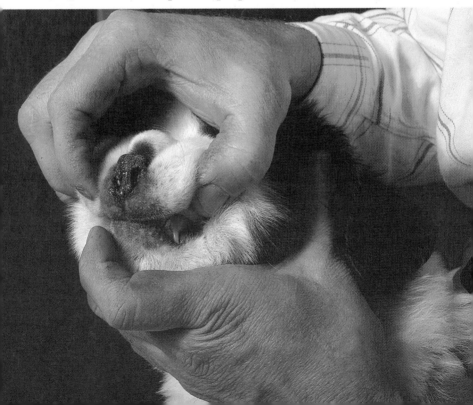

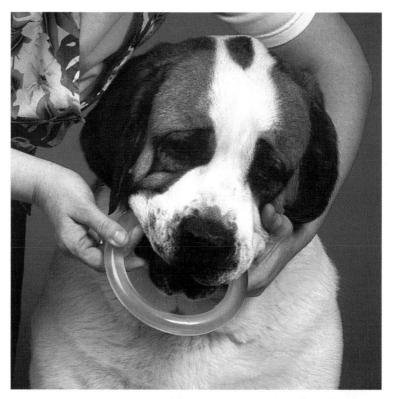

Providing your dog with safe chew toys promotes good oral health and keeps him occupied.

The Plaque Attackers® and Galileo Bone® are other excellent choices for the first three years of a dog's life. Their shapes make them interesting for the dog. As the dog chews on them, the solid polyurethane massages the gums which improves the blood circulation to the periodontal tissues. Projections on the chew devices increase the surface and are in contact with the tooth for more efficient cleaning. The unique shape and consistency prevent your dog from exerting excessive force on his own teeth or from breaking off pieces of the bone. If your dog is an aggressive chewer or weighs more than 55 pounds (25 kg), you should consider giving him a Nylabone®, the most durable chew product on the market.

The Gumabones ®, made by the Nylabone Company, is constructed of strong polyurethane, which is softer than nylon. Less powerful chewers prefer the Gumabones® to the Nylabones®. A super option for your dog is the Hercules Bone®, a uniquely shaped bone named after the great Olympian for its exception strength. Like all Nylabone products, they are specially scented to make them attractive to your dog. Ask your veterinarian about these bones and he will validate the good doctor's prescription: Nylabones® not only give your dog a good chewing workout but also help to save your dog's teeth (and even his life, as it protects him from possible fatal periodontal diseases).

By the time dogs are four years old, 75% of them have periodontal disease. It is the most common infection in dogs. Yearly examinations by your veterinarian are essential to maintaining your dog's good health. If your veterinarian detects periodontal disease, he or she may recommend a prophylactic cleaning. To do a thorough cleaning, it will be necessary to put your dog under anesthesia. With modern gas anesthetics and monitoring equipment, the procedure is pretty safe. Your veterinarian will scale the teeth with an ultrasound scaler or hand instrument. This removes the calculus from the teeth. If there are calculus deposits below the gum line, the veterinarian will plane the roots to make them smooth. After all of the calculus has been removed, the teeth are polished with pumice in a polishing cup. If any medical or surgical treatment is needed, it is done at this time. The final step would be fluoride treatment and your follow-up treatment at home. If the periodontal disease is advanced, the veterinarian may prescribe a medicated mouth rinse or antibiotics for use at

Cleaning your Saint's teeth should be part of your daily grooming routine.

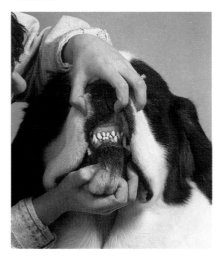

home. Make sure your dog has safe, clean and attractive chew toys and treats. Chooz® treats are another way of using a consumable treat to help keep your dog's teeth clean.

Rawhide is the most popular of all materials for a dog to chew. This has never been good news to dog owners, because rawhide is inherently very dangerous for dogs. Thousands of dogs have died from rawhide, having swallowed the hide after it has become soft and mushy, only to cause stomach and intestinal blockage. A new rawhide product on the market has finally solved the problem of rawhide: molded Roar-Hide® from Nylabone. These are composed of processed, cut up, and melted American rawhide injected into your dog's favorite shape: a dog bone. These dog-safe devices smell and taste like rawhide but don't break up. The ridges on the bones help to fight tartar build-up on the teeth and they last ten times longer than the usual rawhide chews.

Developing good oral habits from the beginning of your puppy's life will help keep his teeth healthy and intact.

As your dog ages, professional examination and cleaning should become more frequent. The mouth should be inspected at least once a year. Your veterinarian may recommend visits every six months. In the geriatric patient, organs such as the heart, liver, and kidneys do not function as well as when they were young. Your veterinarian will probably want to test these organs' functions prior to using general anesthesia for dental cleaning. If your dog is a good chewer and you work closely with your veterinarian, your dog can keep all of its teeth all of its life. However, as your dog ages, his sense of smell, sight, and taste will diminish. He may not have the desire to chase, trap or chew his toys. He will also not have the energy to chew for long periods, as arthritis and periodontal disease make chewing painful. This will leave you with more responsibility for keeping his teeth clean and healthy. The dog that would not let you brush his teeth at one year of age, may let you brush his teeth now that he is ten years old.

If you train your dog with good chewing habits as a puppy, he will have healthier teeth throughout his life.

TRAVELING with Your Dog

The earlier you start traveling with your new puppy or dog, the better. He needs to become accustomed to traveling. However, some dogs are nervous riders and become carsick easily. It is helpful if he starts with an empty stomach. Do not despair, as it will go better if you continue taking him with you on short fun rides. How would you feel if every time you rode in the car you stopped at the doctor's for an injection? You would soon dread that nasty car. Older dogs that tend to get carsick may have more of a problem adjusting to traveling. Those dogs that are having a serious problem may benefit from some medication prescribed by the veterinarian.

Whether you're taking a short road trip or an extended one, be sure to make plenty of stops for your Saint Bernard.

Do give your dog a chance to relieve himself before getting into the car. It is a good idea to be prepared for a clean up with a leash, paper towels, bag and terry cloth towel.

The safest place for your dog is in a fiberglass crate, although close confinement can promote carsickness in some dogs. If your dog is nervous you can try letting him ride on the seat next to you or in someone's lap.

An alternative to the crate would be to use a car harness made for dogs and/ or a safety strap attached to the harness or collar. Whatever you do, do not let your dog ride in the back of a pickup truck unless he is securely tied on a very short lead. I've seen trucks stop quickly and, even though the dog was tied, it fell out and was dragged.

Another advantage of the crate is that it is a safe place to leave him if you need to run into the store. Otherwise you

Car trips can be a fun time for both you and your Saint. However, make sure that your Saint is safe and secure when riding in the car.

wouldn't be able to leave the windows down. Keep in mind that while many dogs are overly protective in their crates, this may not be enough to deter dognappers. In some states it is against the law to leave a dog in the car unattended.

Never leave a dog loose in the car wearing a collar and leash. More than one dog has killed himself by hanging. Do not let him put his head out an open window. Foreign debris can be blown into his eyes. When leaving your dog unattended in a car, consider the temperature. It can take less than five minutes to reach temperatures over 100 degrees Fahrenheit.

TRIPS

Perhaps you are taking a trip. Give consideration to what is best for your dog–traveling with you or boarding. When traveling by car, van or motor home, you need to think ahead about locking your vehicle. In all probability you have many valuables in the car and do not wish to leave it unlocked. Perhaps most valuable and not replaceable is your dog. Give thought to securing your vehicle and providing adequate ventilation for him. Another consideration for you when traveling with your dog is medical problems that may arise and little inconveniences, such as exposure to external parasites. Some areas of the country are quite flea infested. You may want to carry flea spray with you. This is even a good idea when staying in motels. Quite possibly you are not the only occupant of the room.

Unbelievably many motels and even hotels do allow canine guests, even some very first-class ones. Gaines Pet Foods Corporation publishes *Touring With Towser*, a directory of domestic hotels and motels that accommodate guests with dogs. Their address is Gaines TWT, PO Box 5700, Kankakee, IL, 60902. Call ahead to any motel that you may be considering and see if they accept pets. Sometimes it is necessary to pay a deposit against room damage. The management may feel reassured if you mention that your dog will be crated. If you do travel with your dog, take along plenty of baggies so that you can clean up after him. When we all do our share in cleaning up, we make it possible for motels to continue accepting our pets. As a matter of fact, you should practice cleaning up everywhere you take your dog.

Depending on where your are traveling, you may need an up-to-date health certificate issued by your veterinarian. It is good policy to take along your dog's medical information, which would include the name, address and phone number of your veterinarian, vaccination record, rabies certificate, and any medication he is taking.

AIR TRAVEL

When traveling by air, you need to contact the airlines to check their policy. Usually you have to make arrangements up to a couple of weeks in advance for traveling with your dog. The airlines require your dog to travel in an airline approved fiberglass crate. Usually these can be purchased through the airlines but they are also readily available in most pet-supply stores. If your dog is not accustomed to a crate, then it is a good idea to get him acclimated to it before your trip. The day of the actual trip you should withhold water about one hour ahead of departure and no food for about 12 hours. The airlines generally have temperature restrictions, which do not allow pets to travel if it is either too cold or too hot. Frequently these restrictions are based on the temperatures at the departure and arrival airports. It's best to inquire about a health certificate. These usually need to be issued within ten days of departure. You should arrange for non-stop, direct flights and if a commuter plane should be involved, check to see if it will carry dogs. Some don't. The Humane Society of the United States has put together a tip sheet for airline traveling. You can receive a copy by sending a self-addressed stamped envelope to:

The Humane Society of the United States

Tip Sheet

2100 L Street NW

Washington, DC 20037.

Never leave your Saint in the car on a warm day. If he can't accompany you, leave him at home where he'll be more comfortable.

Regulations differ for traveling outside of the country and are sometimes changed without notice.

131

If you are not sure where to leave your pet while you are away, ask your vet for recommendations. He may suggest a boarding kennel or a reliable pet sitting service. Well in advance you need to write or call the appropriate consulate or agricultural department for instructions. Some countries have lengthy quarantines (six months), and countries differ in their rabies vaccination requirements. For instance, it may have to be given at least 30 days ahead of your departure.

Do make sure your dog is wearing proper identification including your name, phone number and city. You never know when you might be in an accident and separated from your dog. Or your dog could be frightened and somehow manage to escape and run away.

Another suggestion would be to carry in-case-of-emergency instructions. These would include the address and phone number of a relative or friend, your veterinarian's name, address and phone number, and your dog's medical information.

BOARDING KENNELS

Perhaps you have decided that you need to board your dog. Your veterinarian can recommend a good boarding facility or possibly a pet sitter that will come to your house. It is customary for the boarding kennel to ask for proof of vaccination for the DHLPP, rabies and bordetella vaccine. The bordetella should have been given within six months of boarding. This is for your protection. If they do not ask for this proof I would not board at their kennel. Ask about flea control. Those dogs that suffer flea-bite allergy can get in trouble at a boarding kennel. Unfortunately boarding kennels are limited on how much they are able to do.

Before putting your Saint in a boarding kennel, check out the facilities to make sure that they are clean and run well.

For more information on pet sitting, contact NAPPS:

National Association of Professional Pet Sitters
1200 G Street, NW
Suite 760
Washington, DC 20005.

Some pet clinics have technicians that pet sit and technicians that board clinic patients in their homes. This may be an alternative for you. Ask your veterinarian if they have an employee that can help you. There is a definite advantage of having a technician care for your dog, especially if your dog is on medication or is a senior citizen.

You can write for a copy of *Traveling With Your Pet* from ASPCA, Education Department, 441 E. 92nd Street, New York, NY 10128.

IDENTIFICATION and Finding the Lost Dog

There are several ways of identifying your dog. The old standby is a collar with dog license, rabies, and ID tags. Unfortunately collars have a way of being separated from the dog and tags fall off. We're not suggesting you shouldn't use a collar and tags. If they stay intact and on the dog, they are the quickest way of identification.

For several years owners have been tattooing their dogs. Some tattoos use a number with a registry. Here lies the problem because there are several registries to check. If you wish to tattoo, use your social security number. The humane shelters have the means to trace it. It is usually done on the inside of the rear thigh. The area is first shaved and numbed. There is no pain, although a few dogs do not like the buzzing sound. Occasionally tattooing is not legible and needs to be redone.

Keeping a collar and tags on your Saint will help to ensure that he doesn't get lost.

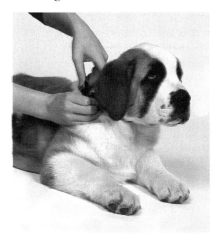

The newest method of identification is microchipping. The microchip is a computer chip that is no larger than a grain of rice. The veterinarian implants it by injection between the shoulder blades. The dog feels no discomfort. If your dog is lost and picked up by the humane society, they can trace you by scanning the microchip, which has its own code. Microchip scanners are friendly to other brands of microchips and their registries. The microchip comes with a dog tag saying the dog is microchipped. It is the safest way of identifying your dog.

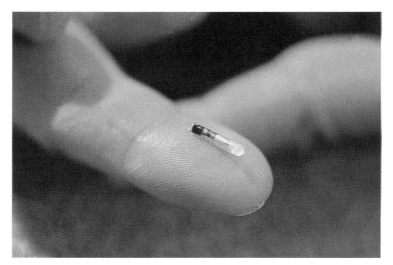

FINDING THE LOST DOG

I am sure you will agree that there would be little worse than losing your dog. Responsible pet owners rarely lose their dogs. They do not let their dogs run free because they don't want harm to come to them. Not only that but in most, if not all, states there is a leash law.

The newest method of identification is the microchip, a chip no bigger than a grain of rice that will help you track your dog's whereabouts.

Beware of fenced-in yards. They can be a hazard. Dogs find ways to escape either over or under the fence. Another fast exit is through the gate that perhaps the neighbor's child left unlocked.

Below is a list that hopefully will be of help to you if you need it. Remember don't give up, keep looking. Your dog is worth your efforts.

1. Contact your neighbors and put flyers with a photo on it in their mailboxes. Information you should include would be the dog's name, breed, sex, color, age, source of identification, when your dog was last seen and where, and your name and phone numbers. It may be helpful to say the dog needs medical care. Offer a *reward*.

2. Check all local shelters daily. It is also possible for your dog to be picked up away from home and end up in an out-of-the-way shelter. Check these too. Go in person. It is

not good enough to call. Most shelters are limited on the time they can hold dogs then they are put up for adoption or euthanized. There is the possibility that your dog will not

Keeping your Saint on a leash when outside will prevent him from becoming separated from you.

make it to the shelter for several days. Your dog could have been wandering or someone may have tried to keep him.

3. Notify all local veterinarians. Call and send flyers.

4. Call your breeder. Frequently breeders are contacted when one of their breed is found.

5. Contact the rescue group for your breed.

6. Contact local schools—children may have seen your dog.

Keep your Saint in a safe enclosed area when he is outside to prevent him from getting lost.

7. Post flyers at the schools, groceries, gas stations, convenience stores, veterinary clinics, groomers and any other place that will allow them.

8. Advertise in the newspaper.

9. Advertise on the radio.

BEHAVIOR and Canine Communication

S tudies of the human/animal bond point out the importance of the unique relationships that exist between people and their pets. Those of us who share our lives with pets understand the special part they play through companionship, service and protection. For many, the pet/owner bond goes beyond simple companionship; pets are often considered members of the family. A leading pet food manufacturer recently conducted a nationwide survey of pet owners to gauge just how important pets were in their lives. Here's what they found:

Studies show that there is a tremendous bond between a pet and his owner. Pets offer companionship and protection and often become cherished members of the family.

- 76 percent allow their pets to sleep on their beds
- 78 percent think of their pets as their children
- 84 percent display photos of their pets, mostly in their homes
- 84 percent think that their pets react to their own emotions
- 100 percent talk to their pets
- 97 percent think that their pets understand what they're saying

Are you surprised?

Senior citizens show more concern for their own eating habits when they have the responsibility of feeding a dog. Seeing that their dog is routinely exercised encourages the owner to think of schedules that otherwise may seem unimportant to the senior citizen. The older owner may be arthritic and feeling poorly but with responsibility for his dog he has a reason to get up and get moving. It is a big plus if his dog is an attention seeker who will demand such from his owner.

Over the last couple of decades, it has been shown that pets relieve the stress of those who lead busy lives. Owning a pet has been known to lessen the occurrence of heart attack and stroke.

Many single folks thrive on the companionship of a dog. Lifestyles are very different from a long time ago, and today more individuals seek the single life. However, they receive fulfillment from owning a dog.

Most likely the majority of our dogs live in family environments. The companionship they provide is well worth the effort involved. In my opinion, every child should have the opportunity to have a family dog. Dogs teach responsibility through understanding their care, feelings and even respecting their life cycles. Frequently those children who have not been exposed to dogs grow up afraid of dogs, which isn't good. Dogs sense timidity and some will take advantage of the situation.

Puppy or adult, male or female, Saints are fun-loving and make great companions for people of all ages.

Today more dogs are serving as service dogs. Since the origination of the Seeing Eye dogs years ago, we now have trained hearing dogs. Also dogs are trained to provide service for the handicapped and are able to perform many different tasks for their owners. Search and Rescue dogs, with their handlers, are sent throughout the world to assist in recovery of disaster victims. They are life savers.

Therapy dogs are very popular with nursing homes, and some hospitals even allow them to visit. The inhabitants truly look forward to their visits. They wanted and were allowed to have visiting dogs in their beds to hold and love.

Nationally there is a Pet Awareness Week to educate students and others about the value and basic care of our pets. Many countries take an even greater interest in their pets than Americans do. In those countries the pets are allowed to accompany their owners into restaurants and shops, etc. In the U.S. this freedom is only available to our service dogs. Even so we think very highly of the human/animal bond.

Saint Bernards are famous for their amazing rescue abilities. Search and rescue dogs are becoming increasingly popular.

CANINE BEHAVIOR

Canine behavior problems are the number-one reason for pet owners to dispose of their dogs, either through new homes, humane shelters or euthanasia. Unfortunately there are too many owners who are unwilling to devote the necessary time to properly train their dogs. On the other hand, there are those who not only are concerned about inherited health problems but are also aware of the dog's mental stability.

You may realize that a breed and his group relatives (i.e., sporting, hounds, etc.) show tendencies to behavioral characteristics. An experienced breeder can acquaint you with his breed's personality. Unfortunately many breeds are labeled with poor temperaments when actually the breed as a whole is not affected but only a small percentage of individuals within the breed.

Inheritance and environment contribute to the dog's behavior. Some naïve people suggest inbreeding as the cause of bad temperaments. Inbreeding only results in poor behavior if the ancestors carry the trait. If there are excellent temperaments behind the dogs, then inbreeding will promote good temperaments in the offspring. Did you ever consider that inbreeding is what sets the characteristics of a breed? A purebred dog is the end result of inbreeding. This does not spare the mixed-breed dog from the same problems. Mixed-breed dogs frequently are the offspring of purebred dogs.

Your breeder should have begun socializing your puppy at five to six weeks of age.

Not too many decades ago most of our dogs led a different lifestyle than what is prevalent today. Usually mom stayed home so the dog had human companionship and someone to discipline it if needed. Not much was expected from the dog. Today's mom works and everyone's life is at a much faster pace.

The dog may have to adjust to being a "weekend" dog. The family is gone all day during the week, and the dog is left to his own devices for entertainment. Some dogs sleep all day waiting for their family to come home and others become wigwam wreckers if given the opportunity. Crates do ensure the safety of the dog and the house. However, he could become a physically and emotionally cripple if he doesn't get enough exercise and attention. We still appreciate and want the companionship of our dogs although we expect more from them. In many cases we tend to forget dogs are just that—*dogs* not human beings.

SOCIALIZING AND TRAINING

Many prospective puppy buyers lack experience regarding the proper socialization and training needed to develop the type of pet we all desire. In the first 18 months, training does take some work. It is easier to start proper training before there is a problem that needs to be corrected.

The initial work begins with the breeder. The breeder should start socializing the puppy at five to six weeks of age and cannot let up. Human socializing is critical up through 12 weeks of age and likewise important during the following months. The litter should be left together during the first few weeks but it is necessary to separate them by ten weeks of age. Leaving them together after that time will increase competition for litter dominance. If puppies are not socialized with people by 12 weeks of age, they will be timid in later life.

The eight- to ten-week age period is a fearful time for puppies. They need to be handled very gently around children and adults. There should be no harsh discipline during this time. Starting at 14 weeks of age, the puppy begins the juvenile period, which ends when he reaches sexual maturity around six to 14 months of age. During the juvenile period he needs to be introduced to strangers (adults, children and other dogs) on the home property. At sexual maturity he will begin to bark at strangers and become more protective. Males start to lift their legs to urinate but if you desire you can inhibit this behavior by walking your boy on leash away from trees, shrubs, fences, etc.

A litter should not be separated until at least seven weeks of age. If they do not begin socializing with people by 12 weeks of age, they will be timid as adults.

A well-socialized puppy will have no problems getting along with other friendly animals. Ch. Heaven Hi's Good as Gold looks after his furry friend.

Perhaps you are thinking about an older puppy. You need to inquire about the puppy's social experience. If he has lived in a kennel, he may have a hard time adjusting to people and environmental stimuli. Assuming he has had a good social upbringing, there are advantages to an older puppy.

Training includes puppy kindergarten and a minimum of one to two basic training classes. During these classes you will learn how to dominate your youngster. This is especially important if you own a large breed of dog. It is somewhat harder, if not nearly impossible, for some owners to be the Alpha figure when their dog towers over them. You will be taught how to properly restrain your dog. This concept is important. Again it puts you in the Alpha position. All dogs need to be restrained many times during their lives. Believe it or not, some of our worst offenders are the eight-week-old puppies that are brought to our clinic. They need to be gently restrained for a nail trim but the way they carry on you would

Establish eye contact with your Saint when giving him a command to let him know that you are the leader. think we were killing them. In comparison, their vaccination is a "piece of cake." When we ask dogs to do something that is not agreeable to them, then their worst comes out. Life will be easier for your dog if you expose him at a young age to the necessities of life–proper behavior and restraint.

UNDERSTANDING THE DOG'S LANGUAGE

Most authorities agree that the dog is a descendent of the wolf. The dog and wolf have similar traits. For instance both are pack oriented and prefer not to be isolated for long periods of time. Another characteristic is that the dog, like the wolf, looks to the leader–Alpha–for direction. Both the wolf and the dog communicate through body language, not only within their pack but with outsiders.

Every pack has an Alpha figure. The dog looks to you, or should look to you, to be that leader. If your dog doesn't receive the proper training and guidance, he very well may replace you as Alpha. This would be a serious problem and is certainly a disservice to your dog.

Eye contact is one way the Alpha wolf keeps order within his pack. You are Alpha so you must establish eye contact with your puppy. Obviously your puppy will have to look at you. Practice eye contact even if you need to hold his head for five to ten seconds at a time. You can give him a treat as a reward. Make sure your eye contact is gentle and not threatening. Later, if he has been naughty, it is permissible to give him a long, penetrating look. There are some older dogs that never learned eye contact as puppies and cannot accept eye contact. You should avoid eye contact with these dogs since they feel threatened and will retaliate as such.

Your dog's body language can tell you how he is feeling in certain situations. Swissongs Morning Glory is nothing but happy to see his friend.

BODY LANGUAGE

The play bow, when the forequarters are down and the hindquarters are elevated, is an invitation to play. Puppies play fight, which helps them learn the acceptable limits of biting. This is necessary for later in their lives. Nevertheless, an owner may be falsely reassured by the playful nature of his dog's aggression. Playful aggression toward another dog or human may be an indication of serious aggression in the future. Owners should never play fight or play tug-of-war with any dog that is inclined to be dominant. Signs of submission are:

1. Avoids eye contact.
2. Active submission—the dog crouches down, ears back and the tail is lowered.
3. Passive submission—the dog rolls on his side with his hindlegs in the air and frequently urinates.

Signs of dominance are:
1. Makes eye contact.
2. Stands with ears up, tail up and the hair raised on his neck.
3. Shows dominance over another dog by standing at right angles over it.

Dominant dogs tend to behave in characteristic ways such as:

1. The dog may be unwilling to move from his place (i.e., reluctant to give up the sofa if the owner wants to sit there).

By standing over your dog and not kneeling down to his level, you are displaying dominance over him.

2. He may not part with toys or objects in his mouth and may show possessiveness with his food bowl.
3. He may not respond quickly to commands.
4. He may be disagreeable for grooming and dislikes to be petted.

Dogs are popular because of their sociable nature. Those that have contact with humans during the first 12 weeks of life regard them as a member of their own species—their pack. All dogs have the potential for both dominant and submissive behavior. Only through experience and training do they learn to whom it is appropriate to show which behavior. Not all dogs are concerned with dominance but owners need to be aware of that potential. It is wise for the owner to establish his dominance early on.

A human can express dominance or submission toward a dog in the following ways:

1. Meeting the dog's gaze signals dominance. Averting the gaze signals submission. If the dog growls or threatens, averting the gaze is the first avoiding action to take—it may prevent attack. It is important to establish eye contact in the puppy. The older dog that has not been exposed to eye contact may see it as a threat and will not be willing to submit.
2. Being taller than the dog signals dominance; being lower signals submission. This is why, when attempting to make friends with a strange dog or catch the runaway, one should kneel down to his level. Some owners see their

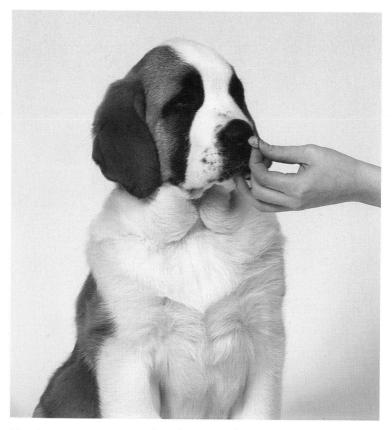

Teach your Saint Bernard to take food without being aggressive.

dogs become dominant when allowed on the furniture or on the bed. Then he is at the owner's level.

3. An owner can gain dominance by ignoring all the dog's social initiatives. The owner pays attention to the dog only when he obeys a command.

No dog should be allowed to achieve dominant status over any adult or child. Ways of preventing are as follows:

1. Handle the puppy gently, especially during the three- to four-month period.

2. Let the children and adults handfeed him and teach him to take food without lunging or grabbing.

3. Do not allow him to chase children or joggers.

4. Do not allow him to jump on people or mount their

legs. Even females may be inclined to mount. It is not only a male habit.

5. Do not allow him to growl for any reason.
6. Don't participate in wrestling or tug-of-war games.
7. Don't physically punish puppies for aggressive behavior. Restrain him from repeating the infraction and teach an alternative behavior. Dogs should earn everything they receive from their owners. This would include sitting to receive petting or treats, sitting before going out the door and sitting to receive the collar and leash. These types of exercises reinforce the owner's dominance.

Young children should never be left alone with a dog. It is important that children learn some basic obedience commands so they have some control over the dog. They will gain the respect of their dog.

Your Saint could experience a period of fear. Be patient and give him time to get used to unfamiliar things.

FEAR

One of the most common problems dogs experience is being fearful. Some dogs are more afraid than others. On the lesser side, which is sometimes humorous to watch, dogs can be afraid of a strange object. They act silly when something is out of place in the house. We call his problem perceptive intelligence. He realizes the abnormal within his known environment. He does not react the same way in strange environments since he does not know what is normal.

On the more serious side is a fear of people. This can result in backing off, seeking his own space and saying "leave me alone" or it can result in an aggressive behavior that may lead to challenging the person. Respect that the dog wants to be left alone and give him time to come forward. If you approach the cornered dog, he may resort to snapping. If you leave him alone, he may decide to come forward, which should be rewarded with a treat.

Some dogs may initially be too fearful to take treats. In these cases it is helpful to make sure the dog hasn't eaten for about 24 hours. Being a little hungry encourages him to accept the treats, especially if they are of the "gourmet" variety.

Dogs can be afraid of numerous things, including loud noises and thunderstorms. Invariably the owner rewards (by comforting) the dog when it shows signs of fearfulness. When your dog is frightened, direct his attention to something else and act happy. Don't dwell on his fright.

AGGRESSION

Some different types of aggression are: predatory, defensive, dominance, possessive, protective, fear induced, noise provoked, "rage" syndrome (unprovoked aggression), maternal

There are many factors that contribute to a pet's happiness, such as a healthy living environment, good care, and unconditional love.

With the proper training and socialization, your Saint puppy will grow up to be an enjoyable companion and good canine citizen.

and aggression directed toward other dogs. Aggression is the most common behavioral problem encountered. Protective breeds are expected to be more aggressive than others but with the proper upbringing they can make very dependable companions. You need to be able to read your dog.

Many factors contribute to aggression including genetics and environment. An improper environment, which may include the living conditions, lack of social life, excessive punishment, being attacked or frightened by an aggressive dog, etc., can all influence a dog's behavior. Even spoiling him and giving too much praise may be detrimental. Isolation and the lack of human contact or exposure to frequent teasing by children or adults also can ruin a good dog.

Lack of direction, fear, or confusion lead to aggression in those dogs that are so inclined. Any obedience exercise, even the sit and down, can direct the dog and overcome fear and/or

confusion. Every dog should learn these commands as a youngster, and there should be periodic reinforcement. When a dog is showing signs of aggression, you should speak calmly (no screaming or hysterics) and firmly give a command that he understands, such as the sit. As soon as your dog obeys, you have assumed your dominant position. Aggression presents a problem because there may be danger to others. Sometimes it is an emotional issue. Owners may consciously or unconsciously encourage their dog's aggression. Other owners show responsibility by accepting the problem and taking measures to keep it under control. The owner is responsible for his dog's actions, and it is not wise to take a chance on someone being bitten, especially a child. Euthanasia is the solution for some owners and in severe cases this may be the best choice. However, few dogs are that dangerous and very few are that much of a threat to their owners. If caution is exercised and professional help is gained early on, most cases can be controlled.

Some authorities recommend feeding a lower protein (less than 20 percent) diet. They believe this can aid in reducing aggression. If the dog loses weight, then vegetable oil can be added. Veterinarians and behaviorists are having some success with pharmacology. In many cases treatment is possible and can improve the situation.

If you have done everything according to "the book" regarding training and socializing and are still having a behavior problem, don't procrastinate. It is important that the problem gets attention before it is out of hand. It is estimated that 20 percent of a veterinarian's time may be devoted to dealing with problems before they become so intolerable that the dog is separated from its home and owner. If your veterinarian isn't able to help, he should refer you to a behaviorist.

Occasionally, puppies may tend to show improper behavior such as biting or barking. Correct these behaviors by using firm but positive reinforcement.

PROBLEMS

Barking

This is a habit that shouldn't be encouraged. Some owners desire their dog to bark so as to be a watchdog. Most dogs will bark when a stranger comes to the door.

155

The new puppy frequently barks or whines in the crate in his strange environment and the owner reinforces the puppy's bad behavior by going to him during the night. This is a no-no. Smack the top of the crate and say "quiet" in a loud, firm voice. The puppies don't like to hear the loud noise of the crate being banged. If the barking is sleep-interrupting, then the owner should take crate and pup to the bedroom for a few days until the puppy becomes adjusted to his new environment. Otherwise ignore the barking during the night.

Barking can be an inherited problem or a bad habit learned through the environment. It takes dedication to stop the barking. Attention should be paid to the cause of the barking. Does the dog seek attention, does he need to go out, is it feeding time, is it occurring when he is left alone, is it a protective bark, etc.? Overzealous barking is an inherited tendency. When barking presents a problem for you, try to stop it as soon as it begins.

There are electronic collars available that are supposed to curb barking. There are some disadvantages to to the collar. If the dog is barking out of excitement, punishment is not the appropriate treatment. Presumably there is the chance the collar could be activated by other stimuli and thereby punish the dog when it is not barking. Should you decide to use one, then you should seek help from a person with experience with that type of collar. Nevertheless the root of the problem needs to be investigated and corrected.

In extreme circumstances (usually when there is a problem with the neighbors), some people have resorted to having their dogs debarked. I caution you that the dog continues to bark but usually only a squeaking sound is heard. Frequently the vocal cords grow back. Probably the biggest concern is that the dog can be left with scar tissue which can narrow the opening to the trachea.

Jumping Up

A dog that jumps up is a happy dog. Nevertheless few guests appreciate dogs jumping on them. Clothes get footprinted and/or snagged.

Some trainers believe in allowing the puppy to jump up during his first few weeks. If you correct him too soon and at the wrong age you may intimidate him. Consequently he could be timid around humans later in his life. However, there will come a time, probably around four months of age, that he needs to know when it is okay to jump and when he is to show off good manners by sitting instead.

Some authorities never allow jumping. If you are irritated by your dog jumping up on you, then you should discourage it from the beginning. A larger breed of dog can cause harm to a senior citizen. Some are quite fragile. It may not take much to cause a topple that could break a hip.

How do you correct the problem? All family members need to participate in teaching the puppy to sit as soon as he starts to jump up. The sit must be practiced every time he starts to jump up. Don't forget to praise him for his good behavior. If an older dog has acquired the habit, grasp his paws and squeeze tightly. Give a firm "No." He'll soon catch on. Remember the entire family must take part. Each time you allow him to jump up you go back a step in training.

Dogs usually jump when they are excited and happy. However, a large breed of dog, like the Saint, could cause harm to a small child. Firmly tell your Saint "No" when he jumps.

Biting

All puppies bite and try to chew on your fingers, toes, arms, etc. This is the time to teach them to be gentle and not bite hard.

Put your fingers in your puppy's mouth and if he bites too hard then say "easy" and let him know he's hurting you. Squeal and act like you have been seriously hurt. If the puppy plays too rough and doesn't respond to your corrections, then he needs "Time Out" in his crate. You should be particularly careful with young children and puppies who still have their deciduous (baby) teeth. Those teeth are like needles and can leave little scars on youngsters. Biting in the more mature dog is something that should be prevented at all costs. Should it occur quickly let him know in no uncertain terms that biting will not be tolerated. When biting is directed toward another dog (dog fight), don't get in the middle of it. Some authorities recommend breaking up a fight by elevating the hind legs. This would only be possible if there was a person for each dog. Obviously it would be hard to fight with the hind legs off the ground. A dog bite is serious and should be given attention. Wash the bite with soap and water and contact your doctor. It is important to know the status of the offender's rabies vaccination.

Your dog must know who is boss. When biting occurs, you should seek professional help at once. On the other hand you must not let your dog intimidate you and be so afraid of a bite that you can't discipline him. Professional help through your veterinarian, dog trainer and/or behaviorist can give you guidance.

Digging

Bored dogs release their frustrations through mischievous behavior such as digging. Dogs shouldn't be left unattended outside, even if they are in a fenced-in yard. Usually the dog is sent to "jail" (the backyard) because the owner can't tolerate him in the house. The culprit feels socially deprived and needs to be included in the owner's life. The owner has neglected the dog's training. The dog has not developed into the companion we desire. If you are one of these owners, then perhaps it is possible for you to change. Give him another chance. Some owners object to their dog's unkempt coat and doggy odor. See that he is groomed on a regular schedule and look into some training classes.

SUGGESTED READING

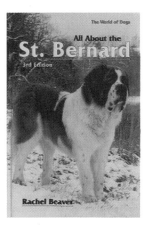

GB 041
*All About the Saint
Bernard
208 pages, over 115 full-
color photos*

TS 214
*Owner's Guide to Dog
Health
224 pages, over 190
full-color photos*

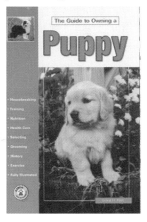

JG 109
*A New Owner's Guide to
Training the Perfect Puppy
160 pages, over 150 full-
color photos*

RE 304
*Guide to Owning a Puppy
64 pages, over 50 full-color
photos*

INDEX

Adolescence, 52-53
Aggression, 152-153
Agility, 22, 84, 101
"Alpine Mastiff," 8
Alpine Mastiffs, 9
Alpine Sketches, 8
American Kennel Club, 82, 103
Barking, 155-156
Biting, 157-158
Bloat, 54
Boarding kennels, 133
Body language, 147-150
Bordetella, 109
Bouritt, M.J., 7
Breeder, 32, 37-38
Bussinger, Stanely, 13
Canadian Kennel Club, 82, 84
Canine behavior, 141-142
Canine Good Citizen, 95
Canine parvovirus, 46
Carting, 22
Characteristics, 23-25
Cohn, Irwin, 13
Commands, 63, 71-79
Companion dog, 24
Conformation shows, 41, 84, 86
Coronavirus, 46, 111
Crate, 67-68, 142
de la Rie, Albert, 6, 12
de Zurlauben, F.A., 8
Deleglise, Prior J., 9
Dental care, 122-123
Diarrhea, 54
Diet, 47-48, 54, 56
Distemper, 46, 107-108
Dog run, 22
Ear mites, 40
Exercise, 62-63
External parasites, 115-117
Fear, 151
Feeding, 54-58
—supplements, 57-58

Fleischli, Joseph H. Jr., 13
Forbriger, Paul, 12
Great Saint Bernard Pass, 7
Grooming, 18, 59-63
Hayes, Mr. and Mrs. A.F., 13
Health concerns, 34-37
Health guarantee, 48
Hepatitis, 46, 108
Holy Saint Bernard de Menthon, 9
Hospice of Grand Saint Bernard, 6
Housebreaking, 64-68
Humane Society of the United States, 131
Identification papers, 44-47
Immunizations, 106-111
Internal parasites, 112-114
Jumping, 156-157
Junior showmanship, 94
Keaton, Buster, 14
Keaton, Eleanor, 14
Keller, Norman F., 12
Kennel Club of England, 82, 89
Knight, Beatrice, 15
Kunali, Dr. T., 11
Laborde, J.B., 8
Landseer, Sir Edwin, 8
Leptospirosis, 46
Lion, 8
Lyme disease, 46, 111
Mallen, Lou, 15
Mange, 118
Muller, Herr, 10
Museum of Natural History, 8
National Association of Professional Pet Sitters, 133
Neuter, 41, 120-121

Newfoundland, 9
Obedience, 22-23, 84, 95-96
Parvovirus, 108
Performance tests, 103
Puppy kindergarten, 84-85, 145
Purebred, 20, 21
Rabies, 46, 108
Saint Bernard Club of America, 13
Salivation, 18
Schumacher, Herr Heinrich, 6, 10, 11
Search and Rescue, 22, 140
Seeing Eye dogs, 140
Seiler, Herr, 10
Selective breeding, 32
Service dogs, 6
Show-prospect puppy, 41, 42
Siegmund, Dr. B., 11
Socialization, 23, 48-52, 63
Spay, 41, 120-121
Spotting, 41
Swiss Kennel Club, 10, 11
Temperament, 20, 32-34, 48-52
The Saint Bernard Classic, 6
Tracking, 84, 98-101
Training, 69-80
—classes, 80
—crate, 67-68
—leash, 71
Traveling With Your Pet, 133
Traveling, 128
Veterinarian, 104-106, 111
—annual visit, 111
—physical exam, 106
Westminster Kennel Club, 90
World War II, 12